Presidential and
Campaign Memorabilia

With Prices

Stan Gores

VH

Photographs by Ted Kremer

ISBN 0-87069-370-0
Library of Congress Catalog
Number   81-52172

10 9 8 7 6 5 4 3 2 1

Published by

Wallace-Homestead Book Company
1912 Grand Avenue
Des Moines, Iowa 50305

To
our presidents
and
all the collectors
they have inspired

Contents

Acknowledgments

Although writing and preparing a book is essentially a lonely experience, the often enthusiastic response and cooperation of others becomes an inspirational and motivating force that transforms the challenge into a pleasure.

Such was the case with *Presidential and Campaign Memorabilia,* right from the time that Don Brown of Wallace-Homestead Book Company caught hold of the idea and triggered it into reality.

As someone who has spent his life writing, I know it is professional to be sedate, dignified, and almost lifeless in making acknowledgments. But I don't feel that way. Those who have helped with this book have given a great deal of themselves and, in the comparatively few words allowed, I want them to know that their individual contributions are deeply appreciated.

Let me begin with the photographer, Ted Kremer, who was always ready to do more than asked and to whom this book is a particular tribute. There was Joe Brown, making his outstanding collection available for picture-taking, lending a series of special photographs, and providing ready counsel on pricing. Jack Putman and Tom Kitchen, friends whom I have known for many years, were equally cooperative in opening their collections for desired photographs and in providing the ready expertise that they have acquired over long years of collecting in the political field.

Herbert Collins of the Smithsonian Institution responded with photographs from the Smithsonian's Ralph E. Becker collection for some of the early presidential illustrations. The staff of Senator William Proxmire, particularly Ricki Grunberg, and the staff of Representative Thomas Petri supplied essential information. Special items were contributed by Marie Stokes, and thoughtful help and assistance came from Gene McLane, Kay Conrad, John Tonjes, Sharon Albright, Pat Schmidt, Mr. and Mrs. Carl Schilling, and many others.

I want to express profound thanks to my oldest daughter, Meg, who spent weeks typing the manuscript, offering helpful ideas, and never once complaining—even when the deadline was staring us in the face. After this ordeal, I know she will never forget our presidents, especially the ubiquitous William McKinley.

Individual thanks also go to others in the family—Paul and his wife, Shari, for items they donated as well as for their keen interest in the whole project; Susan for the gentle way she prodded me to get busy; Carrie for always asking how the book was coming; Julie for letting me make her room a mess with my books, papers, and typewriter; and Jean, Amy, and Sarah for being excited about the book and putting up with me even when I became hard-pressed and grumpy.

And in closing I want to pay singular praise to my wife, Jeannine, who has discovered some of the best presidential items in our collection, who has made some excellent suggestions, and who has been an encouraging force throughout this effort. After thirty years of marriage and eight children, how do you say, for all the world to hear, I couldn't have done it without you.

Did I say that writing the book was a lonely experience? I've never been so wrong.

Introduction

If you can remember the winning smile of Franklin D. Roosevelt or the heartache of watching the funeral procession of John F. Kennedy, you know that presidents touch our lives.

They're not just chief executives, sitting in the White House, far removed from the power of our votes. We put them into office. We replace them. We criticize, or give them praise. We pass judgment on their decisions practically every day. But most of all, we get to know them.

Depending on where we live, we may get to see a president in person occasionally, or we may have to settle for watching him on television or reading about him in books, magazines, and newspapers. Few of us, however, are indifferent to the experience of actually seeing a president. We know we are looking at the leader of a country that is regarded as the most powerful in the world. And he's just plain "Mr. President"—not His Highness or His Excellency.

We have all seen presidents on inauguration day, looking young and vigorous, filled with hopes. We have seen them later, careworn, the victims of strokes, heart attacks, and other serious illnesses. We have even seen them shot down by assassins. And when many of them leave office, we have seen how the job has turned their hair gray, and how the lines have deepened in their faces. It's not hard to understand why the tasks of the presidency have been called awesome.

Because of our partisan views as Americans, we sometimes are happy to see them depart. Other times we are sorry. But whether their record has been good or bad, great or mediocre, they invariably leave the White House scene with a certain amount of our public admiration. As in the case of President Truman, we generally believe that for the most part, on our behalf, they have "done their damnedest."

Over the years, as the office has evolved, our presidents have had some interesting observations of their own about their responsibilities. John Quincy Adams said his presidential term amounted to "the most miserable years of my life."

In his inimitable manner, Abraham Lincoln remarked, "I feel like the man who was tarred and feathered and ridden out of town on a rail." To the man who asked him how he liked it, he said, "If it wasn't for the honor of the thing, I'd rather walk."

William Howard Taft said that as president he felt he was there "simply to hear other people talk."

But to someone as supercharged as Theodore Roosevelt, the constant challenge of the office was such a delight that he commented, "No other president ever enjoyed the presidency as I did."

No matter how our presidents have looked upon the tasks that the electorate thrust in their direction, it has been difficult for us not to respond to them as human beings.

There was godlike admiration, for example, for George Washington. There was a great sense of common man charisma surrounding Andrew Jackson. There was hate, mockery, and in the end, enormous love for Lincoln. There was grief for William McKinley, bully admiration for Teddy Roosevelt, sympathy for the dreams of Woodrow Wilson, sorrow for the shortcomings of Warren Harding, and excessive blame for Herbert Hoover.

The American people, who elected him four times, were lifted with hope by the jaunty, smiling, confident face of Franklin Roosevelt, and believed him when he said, "The only thing we have to fear is fear itself." They grew to understand and admire the gutsy bravado of Truman. They liked Dwight "Ike" Eisenhower, and they shed tears to a sad drumbeat when the caisson moved slowly along Washington streets carrying the body of John Kennedy. Many felt deceived by Richard Nixon, disappointed by Jimmy Carter, and they're still passing judgment on Ronald Reagan.

So our presidents are close to us. In many cases we feel we know them better than the man or woman who lives just down the street.

And because we all share the presidential experience, we are drawn to the thousands of mementos that were made for our presidents during their campaigns and after they assumed office. That's what this book is all about.

It provides a diversified assortment of presidential and campaign memorabilia—souvenirs and trinkets, treasured pieces, and items of contrasting values. But in some way, all have been associated with the presidents and their families. These mementos have been found everywhere—in antique shops, in homes, at flea markets, at auctions, and through advertisements. Some have been received as gifts. Others represent costly expenditures. The majority are from the collection that my wife, Jeannine, and I have assembled over a period of many years, supplemented by items from three other collections and the collection of the Smithsonian Institution. We have always appreciated presidential glass and china. And that, of course, was the propelling interest that sent us hunting for everything else—ribbons, buttons, medalets, postcards, and so on.

The prices quoted in this book are intended solely as guides. It would have been easier to pick a general range, listing a value at $30-50, for example. But we have tried to come up with a single figure which we think is reasonable. In the final analysis, buyers must inevitably rely on their own judgment as to how high or low they want to go to bring something into their collections. As always, the cost of any item is determined by that old cliche, "It's worth whatever somebody wants to pay."

From a personal standpoint, collecting presidential and campaign memorabilia has been a fascinating experience. I'll never forget the day that I was able to hold in my hands a timeworn Jackson flask, studying the rough pontil, looking at the air bubbles, and all the time appreciating that such a glass relic had survived from the time of Andrew Jackson. I felt the same way when seeing a variety of presidential items—a Washington clothing button, a Liverpool jug, a rare ferrotype (tintype), a beautifully colored jugate (two candidates pictured) campaign button. And I know I won't forget the day that Jeannine spotted "Laddie Boy," the handsomely designed metal statue of Warren Harding's famous dog, at an antique show in Illinois.

Of course, learning about any hobby doesn't come without a certain price. I know of no collectors who haven't occasionally overpaid or wish they had resisted buying something. The most dramatic example, in my case, involved what used to be reverently known as "the Jackson frog." This heavy iron bullfrog doorstop, bearing the embossed slogan, "I Croak for the Jackson Wagon," for many years enjoyed a prestigious reputation as a rare artifact of the campaigns of Andrew Jackson.

One interpretation was that the wording meant that the frog was croaking in appreciation of voters traveling by wagon to a Jackson political rally. Pictures of the famous frog appeared in quality history books and in the listings of the most reputable auction houses in America. Moreover, one of the old frogs even was displayed at the Hermitage, the home of Andrew Jackson in Tennessee, where reproduction likenesses of the frog were sold as souvenirs. So I outbid everyone in a mail auction and bought my own, paying hundreds of dollars—as had other collectors and curators before me. But then, alas, in 1980, research by Herbert Collins of the Smithsonian Institution identified the frogs as having been made not for a spirited political campaign from the distant past, but by a Jackson, Michigan, wagon factory in the 1880s! My own checking with a Jackson historian later supported this finding.

So that particular "learning experience," overriding much weighty evidence that had pointed to the authenticity of the iron frogs, came hard not only for me but for many. And like the others, today I accept the reality of simply owning an unusual "advertising item" that is around one-hundred years old and still worth about a hundred dollars as a collectible.

I cite the Jackson frog case merely to illustrate that collecting is a never-ending educational process. Usually the experienced collector will come out ahead. But nobody can own everything. Nobody has the best of everything. And nobody knows everything.

The pursuit of presidential and campaign memorabilia, however, is worth every hour that's devoted to it. If you like history, antiques, collectibles, and the human story of the United States, you'll enjoy collecting mementos of our presidents. And you'll also be joining the ranks of thousands of wonderful people who share the same enthusiasm.

Welcome to an interesting hobby.

Why Collect Presidential Memorabilia?

For every American president there's a trail of mementos. At times, the path may be narrow and almost impossible to find. But the clues of history are there, linked by a huge array of political artifacts that mirror the interesting lives of thirty-nine chief executives—all the way from the worshipful days of George Washington to the bullet-scarred presidency of Ronald Reagan.

Merely looking at a sampling of presidential souvenirs ignites the imagination. An old clothing button shouting the slogan "Long Live the President" tells us of the almost kingly respect given to George Washington. An aged flask embossed with his soldierly profile reminds us of the military character of Andrew Jackson. A paperweight bearing his intaglio image recalls the mediocrity of Millard Fillmore. A campaign ribbon picturing Abraham Lincoln and a solemn tintype of Stephen Douglas kindles our thoughts to those grave pre-Civil War days when, as senatorial candidates, they engaged in historic debates.

Tintype of Stephen Douglas.

An old advertisement from Frank Leslie's *Illustrated* newspaper offering "political goods" such as flags, lanterns,

and torches revives thoughts of dramatic nighttime political campaign parades that were staged for the controversial election battle between Rutherford B. Hayes and Samuel Tilden in 1876. The stiffly dignified features of Grover Cleveland and James G. Blaine, captured forever on time-crazed ironstone plates, stir memories of their emotional, low-road campaign in 1884. The caricatured face of Franklin Roosevelt, embossed on the side of a pottery pitcher, brings back the inspiring personality of the only man ever elected to the presidency four times. And there's a vast assortment of buttons and other items to help us remember those brief, poignant Camelot days in the White House before assassin Lee Harvey Oswald, on November 22, 1963, violently ended the life of John F. Kennedy.

We're carried on this nostalgic flight into presidential history by a bewildering assortment of mementos—pipes, buttons, canes, umbrellas, vases, watch fobs, ribbons, medals, tokens, paperweights, statuettes, pitchers, torchlights, bandannas, postcards, banks, hats, bread trays, jewelry, stanhopes, clocks, posters, ferrotypes, lanterns, bottles, tumblers, serving trays, newspapers, brooches, mugs, badges, and much more. The list seems close to endless. And all of these items now have become treasured remnants of a few exciting moments that flashed and faded in our political history.

Yet presidential souvenirs present a personal record, too. They reflect a time when hopes soared, or great ambitions slowly dissolved in failure, a time when slogans were manufactured to glorify or demolish the reputation of a candidate and, sadly, times when Americans everywhere were cast into periods of deep mourning for a fallen leader. They're often the tattered shreds of days long gone when political parties produced a torrent of colorfully designed items to capture the minds and hearts of voters. But they're also fragments of history that often seem as close to us as yesterday. It's surprising, too, how quickly a president is absorbed by antiquity. And that's why all these collectibles easily fall under the heading of presidential memorabilia.

While there will always be considerable interest in the thousands of fascinating and cleverly conceived buttons that have been turned out for presidential campaigns, particularly the celluloids that were made between 1896 and 1920, far too little attention has been given to the other

THE POLITICAL SITUATION.

An old Thomas Nast cartoon.

delphia moldmaker, P.J. Jacobus (see page 24), are an outstanding example.

While inexpensive sleepers still can be found in nearly all presidential categories, there are certain artifacts dating back to our early presidents—and some rarities from campaigns that came much later—that deservedly elicit extravagant prices. Liverpool pitchers bearing references to or the likenesses of Washington, John Adams, Thomas Jefferson, and James Madison usually bring around $1,300 to $2,000 even when not in the best condition. A sulphide brooch of Martin Van Buren sold in 1981 for $2,500. Scarce buttons and ferrotypes selling for several hundred dollars or more are not uncommon. And also in 1981 at an auction in New York, a 1920 black-and-white jugate button picturing James Cox for president and Franklin Roosevelt for vice-president set a dazzling record when it brought $30,000, plus a buyer's fee of $3,000. The pre-auction estimate of this button, which had sold for $5,800 in 1976 and has been hailed as the only one of its kind, was $10,000. Rarity, condition, the affluence of the buyers, and even the emotional levels of an auction audience are all factors that help determine prices. The smart collector adjusts according to individual circumstances.

So for anyone who enjoys American history or, more specifically, politics, collecting presidential memorabilia is an enormously interesting and educational hobby. It offers the collector the opportunity to specialize in certain elections, or favorite candidates, parties, and preferred collectibles. The choice is determined by whatever a particular collector may find appealing and, to an extent, the amount of money available to spend.

Often the beginning collector can start right at home, searching through drawers, boxes, attics, basements, and storerooms. The discoveries sometimes can be astonishing, especially if a family has shown prior political interest. From there the hobbyist advances to flea markets, antique shops, rummage sales, and household sales. There are antique and hobby advertising publications and well-stocked auction catalogs that are offered by knowledgeable dealers. There are also the American Political Items Collectors organization (APIC) and the Association for the Preservation of Political Americana (APPA), which provide members with well-researched information and the chance to attend state, regional, and national meetings where much buying, trading, and selling is assured. And there's also the challenge of becoming actively involved in the national political convention process itself—where many excellent collectibles originate.

Some collectors, of course, recognize that presidential Americana has been rising steadily in value and consider entering the picture strictly as an investment. After all, investing in antiques is nothing new. People have been collecting everything from folk art to beer cans with a goal of ultimately turning a profit. Nevertheless, most collectors

relics of our elections. Yet the overwhelming majority of them provide fertile territory for collectors.

Most early tokens and medalets have remained "good buys" even though they preceded the handsome ambrotypes and ferrotypes that blossomed during the Civil War era. Medalets made for the campaign of William H. Harrison in 1840, for example, are reasonably priced, primarily because many have remained available. Numerous attractive campaign ribbons dating back to the 1880s are also reasonably priced, while those carrying the likeness of our earlier presidents are generally more expensive. Bandannas, rich in color, still can be found at inviting prices. Message buttons, such as an anti-Franklin Roosevelt pin back that says, "We Don't Want Eleanor Either," can be purchased at far less than many buttons that picture candidates. And certainly glass and ceramics that feature our presidential candidates—their images, slogans, and party symbols—have not been given the prestige they warrant.

Colored elephant and donkey figural bottles, often in their original boxes, turn up frequently from the 1968 campaign between Richard Nixon and Hubert Humphrey. The bottles sell for anywhere from ten to twenty-five dollars, each. These and other comparatively new presidential bottles, made by the Wheaton Glass Company of Millville, New Jersey, are well worth the modest prices usually found on them in shops and at flea markets. In the case of political glassware, in fact, some of the highest quality historical pieces ever manufactured in this country were inspired by presidential campaigns. The Classic Pattern plates designed for the 1884 election by a long-admired but obscure Phila-

known to the author do not rank investment as their top motivating priority. Although certainly aware of rising prices, and delighted to see their political mementos grow in financial stature, they are more enthralled at owning items that they can appreciate from a historic sense. They like knowing that they have something in their possession that dates back to an interesting presidential era. Even an old paperweight showing a picture of the White House can set them wondering who might have been president when the paperweight was made.

Old White House paperweight.

While acquiring all these items and seeing them increase in value, presidential memorabilia collectors also enjoy a fascinating learning experience. A modest achievement, perhaps, but how many friends do you know who can rattle off the names of all the United States presidents in order, usually without stumbling? And how many know the names of the six presidents who held the office in the hectic twelve-year span from 1841 to 1853? Hundreds of collectors recite the list without trouble.

The most effective presidential Americana collectors, in fact, are those who study the history of our elections and become familiar with the names of the candidates—losers as well as winners—and who train themselves to recognize, not only by name but by face, as many participants in our presidential parade as possible. Such knowledge can save many dollars when acquiring a good collection.

To cite a recent example, at a summer flea market in Wisconsin, a seller offered a little clear glass plate with a lacy border. Centered in the plate was the unidentified portrait of a man. The price was stunningly low. After a woman bought it, the seller was curious.

"I've never been able to figure out whose picture that is on the plate," he said.

"It's William McKinley," replied the proud new owner, happy with her underpriced acquisition.

So, as in all fields, knowing how to spot the "good buys" provides the collector with an impressive, money-saving advantage.

This also leads us to those who occasionally are frightened away by the vague observation that prices are too high and "political items are hard to find." The material is still out there, in tantalizing variety, waiting to be discovered—occasionally at bargain basement prices. Moreover, collecting presidential memorabilia allows a smooth blending of the old and the comparatively inexpensive new as presidents come and go in the White House.

Thousands who already collect presidential mementos have found it to be a rewarding, satisfying, and intellectually stimulating hobby. But most of all, it's just plain fun.

Scarcity Years for Collectors, 1789-1828

Acquiring a rare item that dates back to the presidency of George Washington is an extremely difficult and often costly mission. However, collectors are fortunate in that thousands of excellent commemorative items have been manufactured in his honor.

Rarity is not confined only to Washington, however. Just about everything from our first six presidents is in that category. It's true that items from Washington, John Adams, Thomas Jefferson, James Madison, James Monroe, and John Quincy Adams come onto the market occasionally. But since everyone treasures relics from these early leaders, they generally are regarded as first-rate museum quality and are expensive.

Metal clothing buttons are associated with Washington's inauguration, which took place on April 30, 1789, on the balcony of Federal Hall in New York City. After administering the oath of office to Washington, the chancellor of the state of New York observed, "Long live George Washington, the president of the United States." Perhaps as a reference to the chancellor's remark, buttons were made with the inscription, "Long Live the President." There have been reproductions since then, but original buttons in good condition sell for hundreds of dollars today.

After Washington's death at the age of sixty-seven on December 14, 1799, British potters recognized the sales potential among mourning Americans. They began using Washington's image as a profitable decoration on the wares that they exported to this country. As a result, our first president is pictured on Liverpool pitchers, mugs, plates, and platters, Battersea curtain tiebacks, and other items. All the early 19th century items are rare, or at least scarce, and create somewhat of a clamor when offered for sale.

Nevertheless, because he has always remained "first in the hearts of his countrymen," Washington souvenirs have been perpetuated in huge quantities, and hundreds are well qualified for any presidential collection. One side of many early flasks, for example, shows the embossed likeness of Washington, even when the flasks were made to exalt other distinguished Americans such as Andrew Jackson and Zachary Taylor.

Washington match holder from Centennial.

During the time of our great 1876 Centennial, too, there was an impressive Washington boom. The face of our first president appeared on mugs, pitchers, vases, match holders, medals, bread trays, and a wide assortment of other Centennial souvenirs. While these items may not be comparable to the clothing buttons that were worn at the time Washington was still alive, they are already more than a century old and thereby can be classified as antiques. Collectors of presidential memorabilia are wise to look for them and to recognize their status when they are found.

When Washington refused a third term and set a precedent that was to endure until Franklin D. Roosevelt broke it in 1940, he created the first presidential vacancy. It was filled with the election of his vice-president, John Adams, who took office on March 4, 1797. Unfortunately, with the exception of an extreme rarity or two, there is almost nothing to be found by collectors from the Adams' presidency even though he and his wife, Abigail, were the first occupants of the president's house. Incidentally, Adams set a proper atmosphere when he wrote, "May none but honest and wise men ever rule under this roof." Yet despite a dearth of souvenirs, there are ways to fill the gap for the term of Adams, since collectors are able to rely on early lithographs and such items as the aged silhouette pictured in this book.

The talented Jefferson, who history tells us was not an impressive speaker, made up for it with his profound thought and writing, to say nothing of his inventions. Today, those who can afford it try to acquire documents bearing his signature. But there are also Liverpool pitchers and mugs available, and even a rare inauguration medal. Moreover, because Jefferson executed the Louisiana Purchase, numerous items that commemorate that event show his likeness. For the collector, such commemoratives often are not that expensive, yet many are attractive and provide a good representation of the Jefferson presidency, which lasted from March 4, 1801 to March 3, 1809.

President Madison, who served from March 4, 1809 to March 3, 1817, was in office at the time the British burned the White House. His courageous wife, Dolley, saved many valuable articles from destruction, including the famous portrait of George Washington. That episode, in addition to her great charm, is why it often seems that we hear more about Dolley Madison than the president himself. Yet for collectors who can afford them, there are pitchers that portray Madison. Just about anything that collectors can find that shows Madison makes a worthy addition to a presidential collection.

Rarity is also the word for the presidency of James Monroe, March 4, 1817 to March 3, 1825. He is best remembered, of course, for the Monroe Doctrine which was set forth in 1823. There are two mugs that appear on rare occasions, with one spelling Monroe's name correctly and the other listing it as "Munroe." Either makes a prestigious display for a collector.

John Quincy Adams, the only president whose father also held the office, was a winner in the much disputed election of 1824. Although Andrew Jackson led the four-man field with a popular vote of 151,271 to 113,122, no candidate received a majority of the electoral votes and the election went into the House of Representatives. There the supporters of third-place finisher Henry Clay rallied behind Adams, giving him the election. This did all the more to spur on the followers of Jackson, who dedicated themselves to getting him into the White House in 1828. The emotion surrounding this race perhaps contributed to the increase in campaign souvenirs turned out for the Jackson campaign.

Memorabilia from the presidency of John Quincy Adams, March 4, 1825 to March 3, 1829, has remained extremely hard to find. There are some medals, a fabric, a round pewter-rimmed engraving under glass, thread boxes that carry slogans on the cover with a picture of Adams on the inside, and an extremely rare flask that shows his embossed image. Obviously, all these items are costly. However, because John Quincy Adams had a remarkable public service career, he has not been ignored by the souvenir makers. His likeness can be found on paper goods and in a fine Currier print.

By the time Jackson was elected in 1828, the idea of producing more and more political items to promote candidates was on the way to becoming tradition. The American voter was now becoming deeply involved, and many were willing to campaign in an effort to get their man into the White House. Nobody really knew it then, but the colorful political process as we know it today, characterized by parades, speeches, hoopla, and campaign souvenirs, had begun to emerge.

Jackson to Garfield, 1829-1880

Although the candidacy of Andrew Jackson had a catalytic impact on the production of mementos for presidential campaigns, souvenirs from "Old Hickory" have remained somewhat elusive for thousands of today's political collectors.

Jackson, whose two terms kept him in the White House from March 4, 1829 to March 3, 1837, is remembered today by snuffboxes, bandannas, fabric patterns, engravings under glass, thread boxes, clothing buttons, tokens, ribbons, flasks, plates, and some handsome lustre pitchers.

All of these items shout the drama of our early presidential campaign history and, for those who make the pursuit, still can be found. Occasionally, they're discovered in antique shops and, if you're lucky, at large flea markets. But the best sources probably are political mail auctions, where first-rate items continue to go to the highest bidders. Buyers have to be prepared, financially and otherwise, on such occasions because the enthusiasm for collecting presidential memorabilia increases every year.

An erratic pattern that typifies political souvenir production is shown by the shortage of collectibles from the presidency of Martin Van Buren, Jackson's successor. Little Van, our eighth president, defeated not only William Henry Harrison in the election of 1836, but also such a formidable opponent as Daniel Webster, who ran under the Whig party banner.

Among the items from Van Buren, who was inaugurated March 4, 1837, and served until March 3, 1841, are ribbons, snuffboxes, tokens, Currier prints, medalets, anti-Van Buren mechanical cards, and some beautiful sulphide brooches. As in the case of most of our early presidents, the collector has to be prepared to pay well for most items that were made in Van Buren's lifetime.

Many mark the election of William Henry Harrison in 1840 as the real beginning of presidential campaigns. His supporters pulled out all stops in providing paraphernalia to get him elected. It's ironic that he became ill and died after being in the White House for only a month. Until the inauguration of Ronald Reagan 140 years later, Harrison, at age sixty-eight, had been the oldest man ever inaugurated when he took office on March 4, 1841.

His slogan had been "Tippecanoe and Tyler too," which not only served to remind Americans that he had defeated Chief Tecumseh at Tippecanoe Creek, but also boosted the image of his running mate, John Tyler.

Despite his brief moment on the presidential scene, Harrison today is remembered by hundreds of souvenirs, including everything from a variety of log cabin clothing buttons to tokens, silhouettes, cup plates, snuffboxes, ribbons, sulphide brooches, medalets, reverse painting on glass, spoons, bandannas, songbooks, banners, pitchers, lustre pieces, and the well-known Columbian Star dinnerware. Many of these excellent mementos are still reasonably priced and give collectors the opportunity to reach far into the past to enliven their displays with real historic perspective.

With Tyler elevated to the White House by the death of Harrison, it's not surprising that there is an extremely limited supply of souvenirs from his term in office. He became president on April 6, 1841, the first vice-president to fill such a vacancy. Detractors sometimes referred to him as "His Accidency." Tyler's fifty-one-year-old wife, Letitia, died while he was in office and in June of 1844 he remarried, thereby setting another presidential precedent. His second wife was twenty-four-year-old Julia Gardiner.

There's a rare Tyler ribbon and some prints that can be found, but not much else for anyone searching for souvenirs from his years in the White House. However, because he was on the Whig ticket with Harrison, he also shares the spotlight on a number of items that were made when he ran as vice-president in 1840.

James K. Polk, who had served as Speaker of the House and was regarded as an expansionist, assumed the presidency on March 4, 1845, and served until March 3, 1849, choosing not to seek reelection. There are interesting ribbons that recall the candidacy of Polk and George Dallas, who ran as vice-president. Among other artifacts are a songbook, a picture under glass framed in pewter, tokens, medalets, and colored lithographs. Scarcity also keeps Polk items generally high in price.

When the nation turned to Mexican War hero General Zachary Taylor, known as "Old Rough and Ready," the output of campaign items again quickened. Taylor, who served from March 4, 1849, until his death on July 9, 1850, became the second chief executive to die in the White House. He is remembered by a series of flasks, lithographs under glass, campaign newspapers, posters, cartoons, snuffboxes, reverse painting on glass, bandannas, razors, fabric patterns, medalets, clothing buttons, a clay pipe, mirrors, and ribbons. However, despite the variety of these items, they remain hard to find.

Taylor's death propelled his vice-president, Millard Fillmore, into the White House. Fillmore served from July 10, 1850, until March 3, 1853, having suffered a defeat in his effort to win the nomination of his party.

A Millard Fillmore ribbon.

Finding Fillmore collectibles also is quite difficult, although there is a paperweight made by the New England Glass Company, in addition to a pewter-rimmed picture under glass, Currier prints, textiles, a parade lantern,

medalets, ballots, and ribbons. Most of these items were produced for his later unsuccessful bid for the presidency in 1856.

Succeeding Fillmore in the election of 1852 was a Democratic darkhorse, Franklin Pierce, who defeated the Whig candidate, General Winfield Scott. His term of office was from March 4, 1853, to March 3, 1857. Souvenirs of the Pierce administration are scarce indeed, with a field mirror, a few medalets, a ribbon or two, and paper collectibles about all that seem to surface, and then rarely.

In 1856, in the wake of the Kansas-Nebraska Act, the newly founded Republican party nominated John C. Fremont, who was defeated by James Buchanan, a bachelor nominated by the Democrats. During Buchanan's term, from March 4, 1857 to March 3, 1861, tensions continued to mount that ultimately were to lead to the Civil War.

Collectibles from the Buchanan years include ribbons, political tickets, broadsides, flags, and numismatic items. All make desirable additions to any assortment of presidential Americana, as do the ribbons and other campaign items turned out to boost the candidacy of Fremont.

Slavery and sectionalism had become the issues by the time of the 1860 campaign, with the South threatening secession if the nation elected a Republican. The northern Democrats nominated Stephen A. Douglas, with the Republicans favoring Abraham Lincoln. Other candidates during that stormy year were John C. Breckinridge, who carried the banner of the southern Democrats, and John Bell, the candidate for the Constitutional Union.

Home of Abraham Lincoln as it appeared the day of his funeral, Springfield Ill.

Postcard showing Lincoln's home on the day of his funeral.

Lincoln, of course, won the election, taking office on March 4, 1861. He was reelected in 1864. The Great Emancipator guided the nation through the bloody years of the Civil War and preserved the Union. Yet for some, that was not enough. He was assassinated by John Wilkes Booth on April 14, 1865. Although we often remember him as "Old Abe," Lincoln was only fifty-six years of age at the time that he was gunned down—the first of our presidents slain in office.

Almost anything from the Lincoln presidency is held in high esteem by collectors everywhere, and many specialize in Lincoln items. Fortunately, there is much memorabilia from the days of this great president in addition to some excellent commemorative material. There are flags, broadsides, lanterns, songbooks, lithographs, Parian ware, plates, cups, torchlights, bandannas, ribbons, banners, tickets, ambrotypes, ferrotypes, medalets, posters, shell badges, vases, and numerous other items. Outstanding glass Lincoln statuettes, in milk-white and frosted crystal, also were produced by the Gillinder & Sons firm of Philadelphia at the time of the 1876 Centennial. These also merit a high place in any collection.

With the death of Lincoln, his vice-president, Andrew Johnson, a one-time tailor, assumed the burdens of the postwar presidency. His new power soon touched off quarrels between the president and the Republican leadership over the sensitive issue of Reconstruction. Johnson's political enemies started impeachment proceedings against him, but on May 26, 1868, he was acquitted. His term in office was from April 15, 1865 to March 3, 1869.

Unfortunately, little in the way of souvenirs exists from the presidency of Andrew Johnson other than that associated with his campaign as vice-president with Lincoln. Collectors hunt for lithographs and whatever other material they can find to help fill the gap.

Civil War hero General Ulysses S. Grant was elected in 1868 and served two undistinguished terms, from March 4, 1869 to March 3, 1877. Enormously popular when he took office, Grant was not as effective in the White House as he'd been on the battlefield. Newspapers were filled with stories of political corruption. In his campaign for reelection in 1872, Grant also faced the challenge of Victoria C. Woodhull. The first woman ever to be so honored, she had been nominated at the National Woman Suffrage Association convention in New York. Her running mate on the

People's Party ticket was Frederick Douglass, the first black ever nominated for the vice-presidency.

Mementos of Grant's presidency are many and cover just about everything. There are canes, medals, ferrotypes, lithographs, textiles, ribbons, match holders, lanterns, bread trays, plates, Parian ware, badges, jasperware, flags, clothing buttons, posters, and political tickets. Some of the medalets still are reasonably priced, as are "The Patriot and Soldier" and other glass plates.

Adding fuel to the stories of administrative corruption during the mid-1870s, while the nation was preparing to celebrate its first one hundred years of freedom, were charges of dirty work in the election of 1876 between Republican Rutherford B. Hayes and Democrat Samuel J. Tilden. For months the outcome of the voting remained in doubt, with the electoral commission later deciding strictly along party lines to give the disputed vote to Hayes. This was done despite the fact that Tilden had won the popular vote with a plurality in excess of 250,000. Consequently, even though he was not a party to whatever shenanigans might have gone on, the new president was nicknamed "Rutherfraud."

Finding souvenirs reminiscent of the 1876 campaign, which placed Hayes in office from March 4, 1877 to March 3, 1881, is not easy, but many do exist. They include canes, lithographs, flags, mugs, ribbons, ferrotypes, badges, pins, plaques, lanterns, ballots, bandannas, songsters, a miniature toby, and other assorted items. Some of the Hayes souvenirs link his candidacy to the 1876 Centennial and thereby have a double significance for collectors.

President and Mrs. Hayes were the parents of eight children and restored the White House to the good graces of the people, even though there were critics who resented the straight-laced manner in which "Lemonade Lucy" ran the executive mansion. The president and his wife observed their silver wedding anniversary while in the White House and, despite the controversial start to his administration, for the most part Hayes earned the respect of Congress and the nation. He decided, however, that one term had been enough. He did not seek reelection in 1880.

The Years of Plenty, 1880-1912

Having observed the skills and productive capacity of many other countries during the Centennial Exhibition in 1876, factories in the United States had stepped up their own manufacturing tempo by 1880, the year that Republican James A. Garfield was elected president. The productive vigor that they displayed contributed to the abundance of souvenirs that marked our colorful presidential process.

Tragedy awaited Garfield, however, and his days as chief executive were short, lasting only from March 4, 1881 until September 19, 1881. He was the victim of assassin Charles Julius Guiteau who shot the president July 2, 1881, at a Washington railway depot. Yet despite the brief time that he was in office, there are many mementos from Garfield's presidency. Some were made for his campaign, and many were made as commemoratives.

Garfield Drape pattern glass compote.

These include little glass mugs with his embossed image, one with Chester A. Arthur's name on the handle and another with the date of Garfield's death. Found in addition are a martyr's mug on which he is pictured with Lincoln, plus plates, badges, ferrotypes, ribbons, textiles, collar boxes, an ABC plate, a songbook, medalets, Garfield Drape pattern glass, a mechanical nose-thumbing pin, clothing buttons, and a large amount of paper material. Garfield also is shown on a rare pink lustre vase, a delicate but brightly colored Wedgwood pitcher, a majolica pitcher, and a Bennington-type pitcher, among others.

A courageous, well-educated man, Garfield was the fourth president to die in office and the second to become the victim of an assassin. What contributions he might have made will never be known. But on September 20, 1881, his vice-president, Chester A. Arthur, moved into the presidency and served until March 3, 1885. However, Arthur was not nominated by the Republicans in 1884, and there are few souvenirs from his days in the political spotlight. Among items most commonly found are an ironstone plate with his transfer image, produced for the Garfield campaign, and a collar box that also was made for the 1880 election year.

Grover Cleveland, who once had been a sheriff, was the Democratic candidate in 1884, running against the Republican "Plumed Knight," James G. Blaine. General Edward S. Bragg, who nominated Cleveland in a fiery and memorable speech, said, "They love him most for the enemies he has made." But it was a low-level campaign, perhaps the dirtiest in history. Cleveland, a bachelor, was accused of being an occasionally hard drinker, and the nation was shocked by the undenied charge that he had fathered an illegitimate child. Blaine's own marital background was sullied, however, and his political ethics were found to be lacking. He was tagged as being anti-Catholic, even though his own sister was the mother superior at a convent in Indiana. This happened when he did not instantly back away from a remark made by one of his supporters that the Democrats were a party of "rum, Romanism, and rebellion." When this no-holds-barred campaign finally ended, Cleveland had been elected to his first of two nonconsecutive terms. He served from March 4, 1885 to March 3, 1889, during which time, at age forty-nine, he married Frances Folsom, the twenty-two-year-old daughter of his former law partner.

In 1888, although he had performed ably during his first term and had a plurality of more than 90,000 votes, Cleveland lost the election to Benjamin Harrison by virtue of the concept that the electoral college, rather than the people, selects the president.

Collectibles from Cleveland, who defeated Harrison in a rematch in 1892 and served again from March 4, 1893 until March 3, 1897, are not difficult to find. His second term came during the time of the great Columbian Exposition in Chicago, so some things are related to that event. Among souvenirs of Cleveland's two terms in the White House are pipes, bandannas, stanhopes, razors, pillboxes, campaign hats, lanterns, canes, bottles, cigars, match holders, belt buckles, paperweights, plates, pitchers, ribbons, tiles, badges, buttons, and other assorted items. The Classic Pattern glass plates made for his 1884 campaign rank as perhaps the most artistically perfect ever produced.

Harrison, the grandson of William H. Harrison, capitalized on that relationship and revived the old log cabin theme identified with his grandfather in defeating Cleveland. He served from March 4, 1889 to March 3, 1893, when such controversial issues as tariff legislation, the demands of veterans, free coinage, and agrarian unrest dimmed his chances for a second term. Harrison also suffered the loss of his wife, Caroline, who died in 1892. At age sixty-two, he remarried in 1896, taking as his second wife the thirty-seven-year-old widow Mary Dimmick.

Included among the great variety of souvenirs from the presidency of Harrison are well-designed jugate glass bread trays, songbooks, canes, watches, whistles, stanhopes, match holders, umbrellas, a puzzle, cartoons, posters, fabrics, badges, top hats, plates, mechanical pins, tiles, paperweights, statuettes, a bisque novelty item, and many other collectibles.

By the time William McKinley squared off against William Jennings Bryan in 1896 the campaign process was in full sway, including the tactic of using trains for whistle-stops. The first celluloid buttons began to appear, and Americans everywhere seemed to want to wear them to show their political choice. The key issue in this battle was free coinage of silver and the gold standard, with Bryan's "Cross of Gold" speech one of the most famous ever delivered at a convention. But McKinley, campaigning mostly from his front porch, won the election. He took office for his first term on March 4, 1897, and defeated Bryan a second time in 1900 by a larger plurality after the American success in the Spanish-American War. McKinley became the third president to be assassinated when he was shot by an anarchist, Leon Czolgosz, while attending the Pan-American Exposition in Buffalo, New York, on September 6, 1901. He died a week later.

The number of items made for McKinley was immense. Some say that because so many of us have merely stumbled

McKinley gold bug button.

across McKinley souvenirs that he is perhaps more responsible than anyone else for the growing horde of political collectors that exists today. McKinley is found not only on a fine assortment of beautifully colored celluloid buttons, but also on bread trays, pitchers, cups and saucers, ribbons, badges, tumblers, canes, clocks, serving trays, mechanical gold bugs, shot glasses, and bandannas—just to give a reasonable sampling. The same may be said, of course, for the tons of campaign items made for Bryan, who turned out to be a three-time loser.

With McKinley's death, his vice-president, the ebullient Theodore Roosevelt, acceded to the White House. Sworn in on September 14, 1901, he was elected to a full term in 1904 and served until March 3, 1909. Roosevelt helped establish the United States as a world power, and still ranks as one of the most charismatic presidents in our history. An attempt was made on his life in Milwaukee on October 14, 1912. Even though he was hit by the bullet of would-be assassin John Schrank, he still made a speech that same night and went on to a full recovery. Like Cleveland, he came back for another try at the presidency after being out of office, but unlike Cleveland, he failed.

Because of his long involvement in politics, there are many souvenirs that mark Roosevelt's career. Included are buttons, watch fobs, bandannas, serving trays, banks, spoons, plates, banners, flags, pipes, purses, pocket knives, scissors, razors, paperweights, ribbons, pins, postcards, jackknives, Roosevelt Bears items, pitchers, medals, and serving trays. There are so many things to be found from Teddy Roosevelt's time that many collectors just specialize in his presidency.

The last president in the so-called glory years for collectors was the portly William Howard Taft, who weighed as much as 320 pounds and never really was enthusiastic about being in the White House. Inaugurated on March 4, 1909, he remained in office until March 3, 1913. A bright, sociable man, Taft liked to travel and meet the people, a characteristic that added to the many mementos that still can be found from his presidency.

In 1912, Taft faced not only the challenge of Woodrow Wilson, but also the Bull Moose candidacy of his onetime close friend, Teddy Roosevelt. It was in this campaign that Roosevelt coined the expression of throwing his "hat in the ring," and a red and white bandanna made at the time reflects the theme. The Taft-Roosevelt split helped Wilson to victory as Taft departed from a role that he never en-joyed as much as he did his later service as chief justice of the Supreme Court.

In the wide wake left by Taft are many presidential collectibles. Among them are toby jugs made in Germany, plates, banks, tumblers, bandannas, bookends, canes, pipes, paperweights, baby cups, mechanical pins, postcards, watch fobs, stanhopes, tiepins, studs, ribbons, badges, and a fine assortment of celluloid buttons.

But with Taft's presidency there ended a flourishing thirty-two-year period of campaign item productivity that was never duplicated again. Yet much of the evidence of those days remains for all to see—and for presidential memorabilia collectors to discover still.

From Wilson to Reagan

Woodrow Wilson, the scholarly president who was to guide the United States through World War I while driving himself into failing health in his dedicated efforts to secure postwar peace, was inaugurated for his first term on March 4, 1913. Winning reelection in 1916, he served until March 3, 1921.

In addition to helping bring the war to a conclusion, the Wilson administration was also instrumental in producing child labor legislation, supporting the women's suffrage movement, and in pushing through antitrust legislation. But by the time of the 1920 election, with his heroic crusade for peace thwarted, and Warren Harding running for the Republicans and James M. Cox for the Democrats, Wilson was an ailing, disappointed man.

Wilson cigar box label.

Souvenirs of the Wilson era include small china plates bearing his picture, china match holders, buttons, medals, a nutcracker, scarce toby jugs, watch fobs, watches, a metal plaque, posters, badges, jackknives, tiles, ribbons, buttonhooks, cigar cutters, pennants, and numerous other

things. Wilson is a favorite of many collectors, and although a fair amount of mementos were made during his time, they are not easily found.

The team of Harding and his running mate, Calvin Coolidge, outpolled the Democrats in the 1920 election, with Cox and his vice-presidential partner, Franklin D. Roosevelt, losing by a plurality of nearly seven million votes. Harding was inaugurated on March 4, 1921, and served until August 2, 1923, when he died in San Francisco at the age of fifty-seven, weary from a wave of scandals that were still being uncovered in his crony-plagued administration.

Because his days in office were comparatively short, and because not too much was produced for the 1920 campaign anyway, memorabilia from President Harding is not easily found. But there are buttons, cigars, stickpins, purses, tiles, ribbons, jackknives, banners, song sheets, medals, caps, badges, paper items, and the rare "Laddie Boy" dog statue—not to mention those highly coveted Cox-Roosevelt buttons from the losing side.

With Harding's death, Coolidge ascended to the presidency, taking the oath from his father, a justice of the peace, on August 3, 1923, in a middle-of-the-night oil lamp ceremony at his home in Plymouth, Vermont. Coolidge was successful when he ran for a full term in 1924. He was inaugurated on March 4, 1925, and served as America's leader during the Roaring Twenties, when everyone was fascinated with heroes like Babe Ruth and Charles A. Lindbergh. Coolidge characteristically advocated economy and the status quo while the nation drifted slowly toward a period of sharp economic decline.

Although history is rich with photos picturing "Silent Cal" wearing a variety of sober-faced expressions, quantity is lacking among the souvenirs from his years in the White House. There are buttons, a record of one of his campaign talks, badges, medals, pennants, medalets, thimbles, license plate attachments, a pottery savings bank, tiny campaign bells, and posters.

Herbert Hoover began his Depression-plagued term on March 4, 1929. While he succeeded Coolidge when the nation seemed destined for good times, everything changed within a matter of months with the crash of the stock market. Hoover pledged that he would keep the federal budget balanced and promised to expand spending for public works. But people were feeling the financial pinch, and Hoover was made the scapegoat for what happened. Many older Americans, in fact, still remember the Hoover presidency as the beginning of the long Depression and a time of hardship. He was defeated in his bid for reelection and left office on March 3, 1933.

Remnants of Hoover's term are paperweights, toby pitchers, pencils, badges, buttons, license attachments, inaugural souvenirs, thimbles, medalets, pins, bandannas, iron banks, postcards, spare tire covers, celluloid dice, ribbons, stickpins, handkerchiefs, and other mementos, including some highly coveted Al Smith material. Smith was the brash, likeable, and well-remembered Democratic loser in 1928.

Franklin D. Roosevelt bank.

Franklin D. Roosevelt, who introduced much social legislation and was to break tradition by running and winning four consecutive terms, was inaugurated for his initial victory on March 4, 1933. From that day until he died of a cerebral hemorrhage at Warm Springs, Georgia, on April 12, 1945, he remained our president, having won reelection in 1936, 1940, and 1944. Not only did Roosevelt lift the

spirits of the American people, his social programs (and the growing threat of war) helped put the nation back to work. Social Security and labor reforms were introduced during his years in office. He established the "good neighbor" policy in this hemisphere while also aiding our European friends in their task of meeting the growing threat emanating from Nazi Germany. He set America's great productive capacity into motion during World War II and, as that conflict began to draw to a close, was working for a strong United Nations as a means of establishing a lasting peace.

Because he guided the country through the Depression and to new heights as a world power during the war years, there naturally is an abundance of souvenirs from President Roosevelt. They include a large assortment of buttons (many of them not flattering to his disregard for tradition), badges, plates, pitchers, tumblers, license plate attachments, watch fobs, banks, pencils, posters, bandannas, statuettes, ribbons, mirrors, lamps, serving trays, small toby jugs, mugs, neckties, paperweights, and even a cane—the latter an example of a campaign item that was in extremely bad taste, since the president was handicapped. Along with all these things, of course, are some excellent souvenirs from the men he defeated, such as Alfred Landon, Wendell Willkie, Thomas Dewey, and others.

Harry S. Truman, the third man to serve as vice-president under Roosevelt, was elevated to the presidency when Roosevelt died. He was sworn in on April 12, 1945, and, although given almost no chance of victory by the political pundits, won a full term when he upset Republican Dewey after a "give 'em hell" campaign in 1948. Truman made some tough decisions as president including the dropping of the atomic bomb, the authorization of the Berlin airlift, the firing of General Douglas McArthur, and strong action on such domestic issues as possible strikes. He also helped rebuild the war-ravaged nations and, over the years, earned the respect of the world. Today he has retained historic stature as a strong, effective president. Truman did not run in 1952 and left office when his popular successor, Dwight D. Eisenhower, was inaugurated on January 20, 1953. Except for some interesting buttons and a few other items, there are serious limits to good souvenirs from Truman's days in the White House.

An American hero in World War II, Eisenhower served two full terms in the White House at a time when the United States was at the peak of its power as a nation. He suffered a heart attack in 1955, yet ran for a second term in 1956 and polled more votes than he did in his first election. There were minor recessions and heightened tensions with the Soviet Union during the Eisenhower years, but the Korean War was ended and the country remained strong.

There are many souvenirs of the Eisenhower presidency, including ceramic toby mugs of the president and first lady, Mamie, along with such mementos as buttons, cigarette lighters, bandannas, jewelry, ribbons, cigarettes, salt and pepper shakers, bubble gum cigars, a liquor bottle, plates, ties, hats, badges, medals, bumper attachments, rulers, banners, and numerous paper items.

John F. Kennedy, a handsome, forty-three-year-old Democrat, defeated Republican Richard Nixon, who had served as vice-president under Eisenhower, in the extremely close 1960 election. Kennedy had to overcome the political handicaps of youth and being Roman Catholic. Nationally televised debates with Nixon helped him achieve those objectives, and he went on to win the election.

After a brilliant inaugural address on January 20, 1961, President Kennedy embarked upon a strong civil rights policy, created the Peace Corps, pledged the country to an outstanding space program designed to land man on the moon, and forced the Russians to back down during the dangerous Cuban missile crisis of 1962. His difficulties were a disastrous Bay of Pigs invasion in Cuba and his questionable Vietnam War policies. The nation was thrown into a period of deep grief when the young president was assassinated in Dallas by Lee Harvey Oswald on November 22, 1963.

Recalling the Kennedy years for collectors are such mementos as paperweights, plaster busts, salt and pepper shakers, buttons, ribbons, tumblers, cigars, dolls, hats, jewelry, license plate attachments, medals, banners, plates, creamers, and many paper souvenirs. As in the case of Lincoln, Garfield, and McKinley, many memorial items were manufactured and are still being turned out today.

Taking the oath of office on the day of Kennedy's death, Lyndon B. Johnson charted a course that would carry out the civil rights hopes of his predecessor—and history shows that in that regard he did an excellent job. Voters elected him to a complete term by an overwhelming margin in 1964, when he defeated Republican Senator Barry Goldwater. Strong on social reforms, Johnson sought to establish the "Great Society" and also continued enthusiastic support for the American space program. But increasing involvement in the Vietman War splintered the nation, and this factionalism shattered whatever dreams Johnson may have had of seeking reelection. In March of 1968 he announced that he would not run for another term. Three months later Senator Robert Kennedy, the brother of President Kennedy, was assassinated in Los Angeles after an encouraging triumph in the California presidential primary. The Democratic nomination during that turbulent year went to Johnson's vice-president, Hubert H. Humphrey, after a violence-marred party convention in Chicago. Humphrey was narrowly defeated in the November election by Republican Richard M. Nixon who had staged what many regarded as an impressive political comeback.

Souvenirs from the Johnson years include cups and saucers, buttons, badges, ashtrays, belt buckles, plates,

dolls, posters, jewelry, hats, pennants, ribbons, license plate attachments, bubble gum cigars, trays, cloth patches, pitchers, teapots, a clock, creamers, and a variety of other items.

Nixon was inaugurated on January 20, 1969, with Spiro Agnew as his vice-president. On July 20 of that year, astronauts Neil Armstrong and Edwin Aldrin landed on the moon, giving the United States new prestige in space and a boost for the Nixon presidency. However, great unrest continued over Nixon's Vietnam War policies that extended the conflict into Cambodia and Laos. This feeling was heightened on May 1, 1970, when four students at Kent State University in Ohio were killed by guardsmen during a demonstration against the war. The president kept withdrawing American troops from Vietnam, seeking "peace with honor," while also opening important negotiations with China.

But other things also were happening in the Nixon administration. On June 17, 1972, arrests were made and a full investigation promised after a break-in at the Democratic National Committee Headquarters in the Watergate complex in Washington. Later that year President Nixon was reelected, and in January of 1973 a cease-fire was signed to end the Vietnam War. But through persistent reporting in the *Washington Post,* and demands by the press throughout the nation for an explanation of the Watergate episode, evidence began to mount that the president was engaged in a cover-up. There were calls for the impeachment of Nixon, and the Watergate scandal overshadowed whatever else the administration was doing. Vice-President Agnew resigned in October of 1973 on tax evasion charges, and his appointed successor was Gerald R. Ford. Ultimately, Nixon aides were implicated in the Watergate break-in, and as a result of the truth revealed in tapes of conversations that had been held in the president's office, Nixon also was forced to resign. On August 9, 1974, he left the White House.

Although the scandal associated with President Nixon does not make him a favorite of some collectors, his years as the nation's leader certainly were historic. He was the first president to resign and that alone would qualify him as an unusually collectible chief executive.

Among souvenirs from the Nixon presidency are plates, salt and pepper shakers, buttons, badges, jewelry, combs, playing cards, a Watergate pitcher, clickers, bubble gum cigars, cigarette lighters, hats, and a wide array of ephemera.

With Nixon having departed in dishonor, Gerald Ford, by virtue of the Twenty-fifth Amendment, became president of the United States on August 9, 1974. On August 20, he nominated Nelson Rockefeller to be his vice-president and, following hearings, Rockefeller was sworn in on December 19, 1974. For the first time in history, the country had a president and a vice-president who had not been elected to office.

During his comparatively short time in the White House, President Ford reestablished trust in the nation's highest office although he was severely criticized for granting Nixon an unconditional pardon. He offered amnesty to young Americans who had dodged the draft as well as to those who had deserted from the military. President Ford also played a major role in the planning for the nation's great Bicentennial celebration, and sought to rally Congress and the people to fight rising inflation. In addition, he ordered the evacuation of the last remaining Americans in Vietnam and authorized an investigation into the domestic operations of the Central Intelligence Agency. This was not enough to assure him of election to the office he held, however, and in the campaign of 1976 voters—apparently wanting to shake free of all ties with the former Nixon administration—elected Jimmy Carter, a peanut farmer from Georgia.

Souvenirs of Ford's presidency are in comparatively short supply, but they include plates, mugs, buttons, badges, and paper collectibles. As time places more distance between the healing months of dedicated service that Ford gave to the nation, there will be a growing appreciation for memorabilia from his brief administration. And in the years ahead, that should give them added value.

Carter-Mondale campaign ceramic donkey.

Jimmy Carter was inaugurated on January 20, 1977, as an "outsider" with no crippling ties to the Washington establishment. He had made hundreds of promises in his campaign—pledging welfare reforms, cuts in the bureauc-

racy, and a balanced budget. But his performance did not live up to the hopes of the people and he fell steadily in national polls. Carter was plagued by energy problems, inflation, unemployment, an inadequate working relationship with Congress, and divisions within the Democratic party (particularly from those who began to look favorably upon a run for the presidency by Senator Edward Kennedy). Critics of President Carter became more vocal when American citizens were taken captive in Iran and held there for 444 days, despite efforts of the United States government during all that time to set them free. Among his best achievements were his bid to assure peace for the Mideast by bringing together Israel's Menachem Begin and Egypt's Anwar Sadat, and his strengthening of the bonds between China and the United States. He also was regarded as the world's leading spokesman for human rights. Carter sought reelection in 1980, but the national mood was for change—in the person of a former movie actor, Ronald W. Reagan, who scored an impressive election victory.

Many items that mark the presidency of Jimmy Carter were made in the form of a peanut—mugs, buttons, jewelry, and vases, for example. But there were also plates, paperweights, ribbons, watches, umbrellas, badges, peanut holders (or flowerpots), and a good supply of paper and other collectibles.

President Reagan, who at age sixty-nine was the oldest man ever elected to the White House, was inaugurated on January 20, 1981. He pledged a strong America with a powerful military establishment and tax cuts along with a balanced federal budget. It was a big order, with many fearing new problems from cutbacks in the social programs that had grown since the days of Franklin Roosevelt. But in the 1980 election, many Democrats who had been disappointed with President Carter left party ranks and gave Reagan their support. However, his first days in office were marred by an attempt on his life in Washington, D.C. On March 30, 1981, John Hinckley, Jr., a twenty-five-year-old drifter, shot President Reagan outside the Washington Hilton. Following his recovery from a chest wound, the president vigorously demonstrated his political skills in winning bipartisan congressional support for his key programs, although his administration still faced serious challenges from high interest rates, inflation, unemployment, Social Security funding, and foreign policy tensions with the Soviet Union.

The Reagan presidency already has provided collectors with some interesting souvenirs such as buttons, old movie posters, plates, paperweights, umbrellas, a ceramic "jellybean White House," a paperdoll cutout book, a plaster jellybean container (or flowerpot), badges, ribbons, and some rather fancy inaugural items—with much more obviously still to come as the nation's colorful presidential parade continues.

The Presidential Plates of P.J. Jacobus

For decades collectors of presidential memorabilia, as well as glass historians everywhere, have recognized the four Classic Pattern portrait plates made for the election of 1884 as the zenith in historic glass perfection.

Pictured on the eleven-inch plates are the candidates for president and vice-president—Democrats Grover Cleveland and Thomas A. Hendricks, and Republicans James G. Blaine and John A. Logan. Their center portraits are framed within a rim of pointed Gothic panels that feature the familiar daisy and button pattern, and arches that display a leaf design.

But it's the artistic, lifelike detail of the portraits themselves, set against a lightly stippled and frosted background, that makes the plates so unusual. No other images in glass equal these, not even the skillfully made busts of George Washington, Abraham Lincoln, Ulysses S. Grant, and Benjamin Franklin produced in Philadelphia by Gillinder & Sons during the 1876 Centennial, nor the handsome jugate trays of Cleveland and Hendricks and Blaine and Logan, that also were made for the 1884 campaign, nor the similar (but without handles) jugate trays that boosted the candidacies of Cleveland and Allen Thurman and Benjamin Harrison and Levi Morton, for the campaign of 1888. The reason the quality is so high in all these pieces is that they were all created by the same man—a greatly esteemed but little known moldmaker named Philip J. Jacobus.

For years there have been only vague published references to Jacobus as a gifted German moldmaker who was employed by the Gillinder firm. He has therefore remained an elusive figure for glass researchers, and, until now, little has been known about Jacobus the man.

Born in Kreuznach, Prussia, on May 20, 1844, Jacobus came to this country when he was just a boy, in 1851. An older brother, Peter H. Jacobus, who had come to the United States earlier, operated a steel engraving and diemaking business at Third and Chestnut streets in Philadelphia. That's where Philip received his early training and developed his skills as a moldmaker. Old wax letter seals designed by the Jacobus brothers occasionally still can be found.

P.J. Jacobus.

When the Civil War began, Peter Jacobus, who had been an officer in the Prussian army, organized a company of Union volunteers. Commissioned a captain, he entered active service and left young Philip, a teenager, in charge of the business. Much of the money from the work that Philip did was sent to aid the Union troops. That financial drain contributed to problems that led to the closing of the engraving firm. Moreover, Peter Jacobus was wounded in the war, received a pension, and never sought to return to his craft.

But by war's end, Philip had become highly proficient as a steel engraver as well as a diesinker and moldmaker. He had begun to make steel stamps and dies for other companies and, in addition, engraved printing plates for bonds and securities. At one time the United States government sought his talents for the Philadelphia Mint. Philip Jacobus declined, not wanting to work in such confinement. "It's too much like being in prison," he said.

An artist of great curiosity, Jacobus, a thin, bespectacled man with a shaggy handlebar mustache and goatee, kept improving his techniques. He studied many books on the human form and was fascinated as well by the graceful beauty of animals. He was always observing details that helped bring maximum reality to his work. He made molds for desk sets, commemorative medals, and steel statues of birds and dogs. One decorative desk set he is known to have made features animals in a wooded hunting scene. He is credited with being the moldmaker for Gillinder's fine Westward Ho and Lion pattern glass, and his penchant for reality also may be reflected in precise bear-paw handles on the Washington bread trays in the Centennial pattern.

Jacobus, who married and had four children, free-lanced his moldmaking talents. He even set up workshops in the two homes in which he lived in Philadelphia, one located at Twelfth and York streets and the other at 1133 W. Erie Avenue. They were simple workshops, with just a bench and some tools, but they provided a place for him to toil on a variety of assignments that kept him busy and earning a living.

Wesley I. Slagle of Philadelphia, a great-grandson of the moldmaker, told me that Jacobus made molds for the expositions that were held in Chicago in 1893 and in St. Louis in 1904. Slagle also owns "a signed plate" from the St. Louis Exposition. In addition, he has two beer mugs decorated with the images of early baseball players. Both of the baseball mugs have cooling cracks, however, since they are believed to be the first examples poured, and revealed a production flaw. Along with his talents as a moldmaker, Jacobus also enjoyed painting. He found creative satisfaction in painting mountain scenes in clamshells, emphasizing the same attention to detail that he displayed in sculpting molds for glass.

But of all the objects he may have created or beautified, Jacobus, who died on January 23, 1910, at the age of sixty-five after suffering a stroke, is best remembered today for the molds he designed for the Gillinder firm. The company gained world recognition during the 1876 Centennial by setting up a complete glassmaking operation right on the grounds in Philadelphia. It was at that time that Jacobus fashioned the fine acid-finish busts of Washington, Lincoln, and Grant in both clear and milk glass that presidential collectors now seek.

Yet in the author's opinion, the peak of his moldmaking artistry is exemplified in the Classic Pattern plates that Jacobus, in collaboration with John Putnam, made for the 1884 election. These were extraordinary molds of Cleveland, Hendricks, Blaine, and Logan, showing details in the hair and eyebrows, facial expressions, sensitivity in the eyes, lines and wrinkles in the skin, and clothing so carefully copied that if colored it would look like real cloth. They capture in beautiful clear-frosted glass a political campaign that often was characterized by the cartoonists of the day and by the contemporary press as a period of mudslinging. Jacobus apparently didn't see the campaign with such limited vision. He saw four interesting faces—and four human beings—and that's what he duplicated for history, even better than a camera could have done.

Little wonder then, after putting so much of himself into each work of art, that he signed the Hendricks and Blaine plates in his characteristic way, "P.J. Jacobus, scul."

Time has shown that Jacobus was indeed much more than a moldmaker.

Presidential Memorabilia
with Prices

George Washington
1789-1797

George Washington is shown in color in this reverse painting on glass which appears on a little patch box dating from the 1840s. The glass is bordered by gold paper trim, and beneath the cover is a mirror. The sides of the box are made to look like pages in a closed book. On the reverse side of the 2¾″ × 1¾″ glass-covered box is the reminder, "Forget Me Not."

$225

Americans elevated George Washington to almost divine status, so it was appropriate that Liverpool pitchers were decorated with a heavenly theme. This Apotheosis pitcher shows Washington amid angelic surroundings, height, 8″.

$1,500

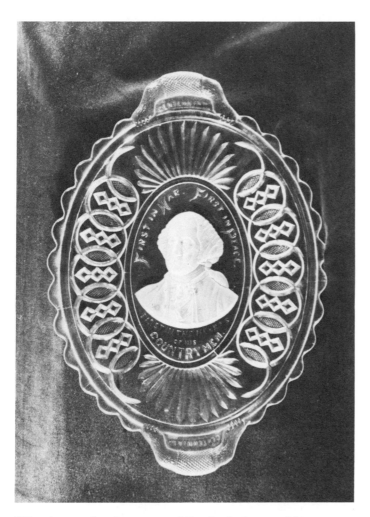

Clothing buttons made for the presidency of George Washington today have become rare collectibles. Those shown bear the initials "GW" in the center and carry the wording, "Long Live the President." Over the years, Washington buttons have been reproduced, so buyers must learn to distinguish the old from those that were manufactured later. As we approach the bicentennial of Washington's inauguration, the original clothing buttons can be expected to increase in value.

(L) **$550**
(C) **$700**
(R) **$850**

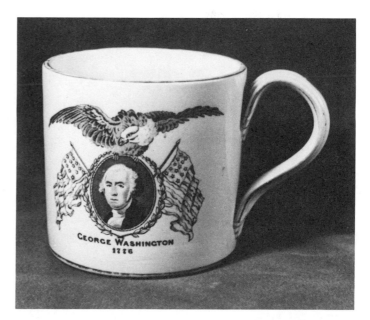

"First in war, first in peace, and first in the hearts of his countrymen." The familiar quotation associated with George Washington appeared on bread plates honoring our first president at the time of the 1876 Centennial. This one shows the image of Washington frosted, but the heavy tray also was made in all-clear and all-frosted glass. The bearpaw handles are embossed "Centennial" and carry the 1776 and 1876 dates. Made by Gillinder & Sons of Philadelphia, length, 12".

$125

George Washington was well remembered at the time of the 1876 Centennial, and this china mug with American flags, eagle, and Washington's framed countenance is a good example. Made by W.T. Copeland & Sons for J.M. Shaw & Company of New York, such mugs and cups were sold as Centennial souvenirs. Washington's name and "1776" are on one side. The other side reads, "A Memorial of the Centennial, 1876." The cup measures 3" in height. On some of the mugs and cups the illustration is in color.

$75

27

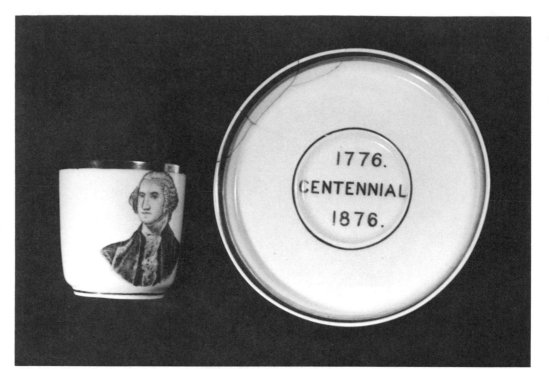

A demitasse cup and saucer were made at the time of the 1876 Centennial to honor the memory of our first president. The top and base of the tiny cup are trimmed with gold. The plate is dated 1776-1876. Attributed to Onodaga Pottery Company, Syracuse, New York. The cup is 2¼″ high, and the diameter of the saucer is 4¼″.

$75

The Houdon bust of George Washington is highlighted in this medallion paperweight made by Gillinder & Sons of Philadelphia for the 1876 Centennial. The sides, upper edging and intaglio image of Washington are acid-treated to contribute to the impressive contrast. Diameter, 3″, height, 1″. An excellent paperweight.

$140

The special place that George Washington will always have in American history is reflected on this plate, made for the 1876 Centennial. The flags are in color, and the border of the 6″ plate is embossed with the words, "Our Union Forever" and "Centennial."

$95

George and Martha Washington appear as tintypes on this silver-plated belt buckle sold at the time of the Centennial in 1876. The buckle is 2⅛″ high and 3¼″ wide. A good Americana piece.

$75

During the Columbian Exposition in Chicago in 1893 George Washington was honored, along with Columbus, in a variety of ways. Here our first president is pictured on a beautiful Doulton Lambeth pitcher which stands 7″ high and is decorated in cobalt blue. Washington's year of birth and age at death are in the frame around his bas-relief image. The pitcher also carries the embossed likeness of Columbus and the American eagle, and is dated, "World's Columbian Exposition 1893."

$275

A Stevengraph bookmark, honoring the memory of George Washington and made at the time of the nation's Centennial celebration in 1876, is shown on the right, displayed under glass. Another beautifully colored Washington bookmark, made around the same time, is pictured on the left. Both are about 10″ long.

Stevengraph **$135**
Unsigned bookmark **$90**

John Adams
1797·1801

Little ceramic mugs were made to honor the presidency of John Adams. His image and his name appear on one, while the other emphasizes the Adams name within a floral border topped by the American eagle. The mugs probably were made before 1820, height, 2½″.

Picture mug **$1,300**
Eagle mug **$850**

John Adams is shown in this gold and black silhouette on glass, with the name of the president written in signature form within the bottom border, probably made before 1840. The wooden frame is 7⅛″ × 8⅛″.

$150

Thomas Jefferson
1801-1809

Thomas Jefferson's inaugural address is carried on the second page of this March 16, 1801, edition of the Boston Gazette. A man of immense ability, Jefferson displayed his humility when he remarked that he had "a sincere consciousness that the task is above my talents." He also asked members of Congress for their "guidance and support." The same issue contains references to John Hancock, James Madison, and others of early prominence. The paper is tabloid size.

$65

rather heavy-handed transfer image of ...ies him as "President of the United ...same transfer appears on other items, ...her. Collectors need not worry too much ...types of presidential relics come along.

$1,250

Buildings made for the World's Fair in St. Louis in 1904 are featured on the border of this blue and white plate which honors President Thomas Jefferson, "Father of the Louisiana Purchase." The Rowland and Marsellus Company plate was designed and imported by Barr's of St. Louis for the World's Fair, diameter, 10".

$60

James Monroe
1817-1825

The potters misspelled the name of President James Monroe when they made this little 2½″ mug featuring a floral and eagle design. The error adds to the interest, and shows that English craftsmen were more attuned to selling than they were to accuracy in producing presidential souvenirs for the American market. Similar to one of the mugs made for John Adams. Scarce.

$800

James Madison
1809-1817

An old silhouette, painted on glass in gold and decorated with black for details, honors President James Madison. This is a companion silhouette to the one picturing John Adams, with the name shown in signature form in the gold rectangle below the profile of Madison. The wooden frame is 7⅛″ × 8⅛″.

$150

John Quincy Adams
1825-1829

A picture of John Quincy Adams adorns the inside of the lid of this little sewing box that was made as a campaign item for the election of 1824. The sides are decorated in rainbow colors and the top and bottom edges feature gold paper trim. The tops of these boxes carried such slogans as "Adams Forever" and "Victory for Adams." Excellent presidential relics, and rare.

$1,100

John Quincy Adams was among the early presidents pictured in the colored lithographs of N. Currier. Shown behind glass in an old wooden frame of the period that measures 14¼" × 16¼". Adams is identified as the "6th President of the United States." There were many presidential prints made by N. Currier and Currier & Ives, and all are growing in value.

$100

Andrew Jackson
1829-1837

Andrew Jackson is pictured as "The Hero of New Orleans" on this handsome lustre pitcher that probably served as a campaign item back in 1828. Such pieces are rare and, like this one from the Smithsonian Institution, often wind up in a museum—or on display in the home of a lucky collector.

$1,100

Two presidential numismatic items from the days of Andrew Jackson are shown, with the larger circulated at the time of his 1828 campaign against John Quincy Adams and the other used in 1832 when he defeated Henry Clay. Other tokens and medalets were also made. Since prices vary, collectors should study numismatics to become familiar with the field.

1828	**$400**
1832	**$150**

This Andrew Jackson portrait flask, made by the Keene Glass Works of New Hampshire in 1828 for his campaign against John Quincy Adams, is 6¾" in height and dark olive green in color. Above his embossed image is the name "JACKSON," with a portrait of Washington on the other side. Only five of our presidents are pictured on the early flasks—Washington, John Quincy Adams, Jackson, William H. Harrison, and Zachary Taylor. Eleven different molds were used for the Jackson flasks, and all are scarce.

$300

Will the real Jackson frog please stand up? If that question could be asked of these iron doorstops embossed with the wording, "I croak for the Jackson Wagon," they'd have to remain in place. For years the old iron frogs were considered treasures from the campaign of Andrew Jackson, and brought prices of up to $700. Then Herbert Collins of the Smithsonian Institution, writing in *The Keynoter* publication of the American Political Items Collectors, Spring 1980 issue, disclosed that his research had revealed them to be the early 1880s advertising gimmicks of a Jackson, Michigan, wagon company. The frog on the left is an old example. The one on the right, however, was purchased as a souvenir from Jackson's historic Hermitage for under $10. The old frogs still have value as advertising doorstops—but have lost much of their glamour. They are 3″ high, 5½″ long.

$100

Martin Van Buren
1837-1841

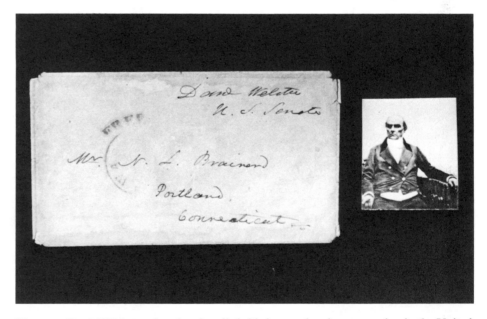

The great Daniel Webster signed and mailed this letter when he was serving in the United States Senate. Striking in appearance, Webster was among the most gifted leaders and orators this country ever produced. Yet even though he was a Whig presidential candidate in 1836, the presidency always eluded him. The reverse side of the letter shown carries Webster's black seal, with the initials "DW." Webster is pictured next to the letter, which is 5¼″ × 3″ in size.

$75

A rare ribbon from the days of Martin Van Buren also pictures Washington, Jefferson, and Jackson. The well-decorated presidential artifact is 7½″ long and 2½″ wide. A highly desirable memento, it captures the political drama of an interesting era.

$1,200

William Henry Harrison
1841

"Harrison and Reform" was one of the slogans in the lively 1840 campaign when the backers of General Harrison went all out to get their man elected. This beautiful copper lustre pitcher, which shows the candidate, was made for the campaign. With its graceful design, the pitcher is a rarity that any presidential collector would treasure.

$1,100

The log cabin theme and military background were emphasized in this attractive campaign ribbon made for William H. Harrison in his 1840 race against Martin Van Buren. The ribbon is 6½" long and 2½" wide.

$150

Although he died after only one month in office, William H. Harrison today is remembered by an enormous amount of interesting memorabilia. This item is a cup plate showing Harrison and listing the date of his birth, while also carrying the identification "President" and the year, "1841." The plate was made by the Boston & Sandwich Glass Factory. Harrison was the first president to die while serving in the White House. The diameter of the plate is 3½".

$50

William H. Harrison's log cabin and barrel of hard cider campaign touched off the production of Columbian Star tableware, decorated with a log cabin and cider barrel in a tranquil rural setting. This is a handle-less cup, but there also are many other attractive pieces. China made for the Harrison campaign came in several colors, and some pieces were adorned with the medallion likeness of Harrison. The cup shown here is 2¼" in height.

$70

John Tyler
1841·1845

Finding anything from the presidency of John Tyler is a challenge, although a rare ribbon appears on the market from time to time. He was fifty-one when inaugurated, taking office upon the death of William H. Harrison, with whom he ran as vice-president on the Whig ticket in 1840. Tyler, who married twice, had fifteen children. He is shown here in an old lithograph.

$12

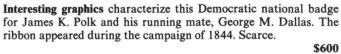

Interesting graphics characterize this Democratic national badge for James K. Polk and his running mate, George M. Dallas. The ribbon appeared during the campaign of 1844. Scarce.

$600

Henry Clay looks youthful on this interesting leather cigar-holder made as a campaign item in 1844. The holder is pictured along with the insert. Clay is identified as "The American Statesman." A scarce artifact that is 5½" long and 3" wide.

$475

Henry Clay's bid for the presidency in 1844 as the Whig party candidate against James K. Polk produced this interesting old clay pipe. It carries the identification "Henry Clay" and shows his embossed features. One side of the stem has the wording, "Warranted to color." A surprising number of these old pipes have survived. The bowl is 2½″ high.

$60

Henry Clay is described as the "Protector of American Industry" on this well-illustrated campaign ribbon. The Clay campaign of 1844 stressed his support for American industry in many ways, but the people seemed more in tune with the expansionist ideas of Polk. The ribbon is 7½″ long.

$150

Zachary Taylor
1849-1850

General Zachary Taylor flask, made by the Dyottville Glass Works, Philadelphia, in 1848 for Taylor's presidential campaign. The aquamarine flask carries Taylor's embossed image, showing five buttons on his coat, and emphasizes the courageous slogan, "Gen. Taylor Never Surrenders." The other side pictures George Washington, "The Father of His Country." Although not easily found, Taylor flasks come in twenty-eight variations, height, 7¼″.

$130

Millard Fillmore
1850-1853

Millard Fillmore appears on this early presidential paperweight, made by the New England Glass Company of East Cambridge, Massachusetts. It was probably produced in late 1850, since Fillmore was in office only from the time of Zachary Taylor's death until 1852. Moreover, the inscription surrounding his frosted intaglio image identifies him as "Millard Fillmore, President of the United States" and carries the "1850" date beneath his portrait. Hexagonal in shape, the Fillmore weight was made in limited quantity and is considered rare. It has beveled edges, is 3½″ wide and nearly 1″ high. **$300**

Franklin Pierce
1853-1857

A rare jugate ribbon from the 1852 campaign is shown here. It pictures Franklin Pierce and William R. King, the successful Democratic party candidates. Few collectors are able to display such a prize in their collections. The ribbon is 6½″ long, 2½″ wide. **$2,000**

Made while he was in office, this battered field mirror with the pewter case pictures "General Franklin Pierce, President of the United States." Highly valued by presidential collectors, it is extremely hard to find. A similar mirror also was made for Zachary Taylor. **$265**

Crusty-looking Winfield Scott is shown on this great old lithograph published by A. Winch, 320 Chestnut Street, Philadelphia. The Whigs preferred Scott as their candidate in 1852 rather than the incumbent president, Millard Fillmore. Scott lost the election to Pierce by around 215,000 votes. The framed lithograph measures 17½″ × 13½″.

$100

General Winfield Scott is pictured on an ABC plate that helped promote his campaign for the presidency. The platemaker spelled his first name incorrectly, but that rather common problem just adds interest to this memento. Diameter, 5″.

$170

James Buchanan
1857-1861

The Buchanan-Breckinridge Democratic ticket is pictured on this paper ballot, along with a listing of "our principles"—which included a pledge to repeal the "Missouri Restriction." Unusual graphics make this an interesting collectible.

$40

Described as the "Birthplace of the Republican Party," a little schoolhouse in Ripon, Wisconsin, is pictured on these two pieces of souvenir china. The GOP was founded in 1854 and made John Fremont its first candidate for the White House. Their second candidate—Abraham Lincoln—was elected in 1860. The vase is 5″ tall; the creamer measures 3¾″.

Each **$25**

A campaign ribbon picturing James Buchanan for the election of 1856 not only lists the name of his running mate, John C. Breckinridge, but also adds a touch of humor with the words, "We Po'ked 'em in '44, We Pierced 'em in '52, And we'll 'Buck 'em' in '56." Length, 7″.

$170

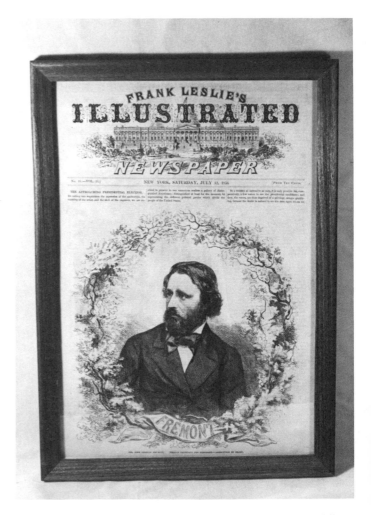

John Charles Fremont was the first candidate of the Republican party in the presidential election of 1856. An explorer, army officer, and politician, Fremont made an attractive candidate but lost to Buchanan by about 500,000 votes. He is shown here in a framed cover of Frank Leslie's *Illustrated,* dated July 12, 1856. Fremont's likeness is identified as having been "Ambrotyped by Brady."

$25

The first presidential candidate of the new Republican party is shown on this medalet turned out to win votes for John C. Fremont. The medalet is 1⅛″ in diameter, and its message advocates "Free Soil, Free Speech."

$28

Losers in the presidential race in 1856 were John C. Fremont and Millard Fillmore, the latter running as the candidate of the American party, the "Know Nothings." The Fremont ribbon is 5″ in length, while the Fillmore ribbon measures 7¼″.

Fremont **$80**
Fillmore **$135**

Abraham Lincoln
1861·1865

Six ferrotypes from the 1860 presidential election are pictured in this lineup. From left to right, they show Lincoln; Lincoln and Hamlin; Douglas; Breckinridge and Lane; Breckinridge; and Bell. All are sought after by collectors.

Lincoln	$190	Breckinridge-Lane	$1,100
Lincoln-Hamlin	$950	Breckinridge	$130
Douglas	$475	Bell	$600

The Honorable Hannibal Hamlin is shown on this transfer souvenir china plate made in Germany for the Adams and Strickland firm of Bangor, Maine. The plate probably dates from before the turn of the century. Hamlin served as Lincoln's vice-president during his first term. Diameter, 5½″.

$75

Mathew Brady portrait ribbons were made for candidates in the 1860 election and this beauty, complete with facsimile signature, features the inspiring likeness of Abraham Lincoln. Others found on the Brady single-picture ribbons include John Breckinridge, Stephen Douglas, and John Bell. The Lincoln ribbon is 6½″ long, 2½″ wide. Scarce.

$575

Mary Todd Lincoln, a somewhat tragic figure in American history, is pictured in color on this plate, one in a series believed made around 1909, during Lincoln's Centennial. Although the plate, probably a giveaway, is not high quality china, it is attractive and an appropriate addition to a presidential collection. The back is marked "Imperial China" and "a remembrance from Zander-Pfeffer Co." It is 6″ square.

$15

Stephen A. Douglas, defeated by Abraham Lincoln in the 1860 presidential race, is remembered by this unusual handleless cup that shows his birthplace in Brandon, Vermont. An extremely delicate ceramic souvenir, the cup was made for the Charles H. Ross retail outlet in Brandon. It stands 2¼″ high.

$50

The dramatic setting for Abraham Lincoln's Gettysburg address is pictured on these two items made by the Homer Laughlin China Company for the firm's Historical America china set. Lincoln, shown talking to the crowd, is pictured in red on both sides of the gravy boat, which measures 8½″ long and 3⅜″ high. The serving bowl, which also has a red floral border, is 9½″ × 7″.

Gravy boat **$60**
Serving bowl **$35**

Jefferson Davis, who served as president of the Confederacy at the time of the Civil War, is embossed in the center of this attractive amber plate, produced by the L.E. Smith Glass Company, Mount Pleasant, Pennsylvania. Made in 1960, it also can be found in milk-white glass. Diameter, 9¼″.

$25

45

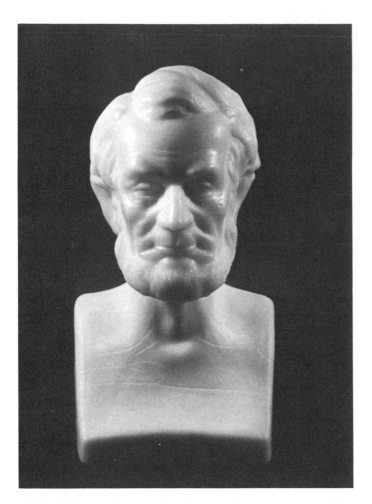

Abraham Lincoln is honored in this expertly sculptured, acid-finish milk-white glass bust designed by P.J. Jacobus for Gillinder & Sons of Philadelphia at the time of the 1876 Centennial. The 6¼" bust has a hollow base, while others are solid and bear Centennial markings. It is also found in clear glass with an acid finish. At the time of the Centennial the busts wholesaled at $.75 each. Because of the fine workmanship and Lincoln's place in history they now are highly prized by collectors.

$400

"Lincoln at Home" is the name given to this Currier & Ives lithograph produced in 1867. It shows Mrs. Lincoln, Robert Lincoln, Tad, and the President. Still in the original 14" × 17" frame.

$100

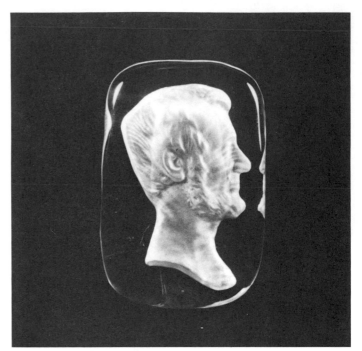

Abraham Lincoln collectors always have admired this heavy rectangular weight with the intaglio likeness of the great Civil War president. Good clear glass, and a frosted finish on Lincoln's features. Believed made sometime between the 1876 Centennial and 1900. It is 4⅜" long, 3" wide.

$110

This rather unusual Lincoln plate was made for a gathering of the Lincoln Park Chapter No. 177, Royal Arch Masons, in Chicago on February 12, 1910. Decorated in color with Lincoln's image and his birthplace, it features a letter President Lincoln wrote to Mrs. Bixby in Boston in 1864. Mrs. Bixby lost five sons in the Civil War. Lincoln's letter to her has been called an example of the "purest English" ever written. A fine collectible plate. Diameter, 8½".

$35

The bas-relief likeness of Lincoln appears in white on a blue tile made by the Allen Tiling Company of Chicago. It is 3″ high, 3⅜″ wide.

$20

Some confusion exists regarding this full-color portrait plate of Abraham Lincoln. Actually, it is believed to date to around 1909, the time of the Lincoln Centennial, with one attribution listing it as a giveaway by the Teeds China Emporium. The reverse side shows an image believed to be the Liberty Bell, topped by the head of an eagle. Inside the bell is the marking, "The Colonial Co." A fine presidential memento. Diameter, 8¼″.

$48

A smiling Lincoln is featured in this round paperweight made eleven years after his death by the Gillinder & Sons glass firm on the grounds of the 1876 Centennial in Philadelphia. The sides, the upper edge, and the intaglio impression of the Great Emancipator are acid-treated, or as many say, "frosted." A fine glass souvenir of a great president. The diameter is 3″, the height 1″.

$150

Lincoln's image is deeply impressed in the base of this oval paperweight made by Gillinder & Sons of Philadelphia and sold at the time of the nation's Centennial celebration in 1876. The bottom and sides were treated with acid, with the top polished so as to emphasize Lincoln's features. The paperweight is 5½″ long, 4″ wide. An excellent piece of historical glass.

$210

A rare paper campaign lantern from 1864 when George McClellan, pictured on the lantern, opposed Abraham Lincoln. It is remarkable that such a delicate presidential artifact could survive, thus adding to its rarity. In addition to the obvious printing on the lantern, the other sides called for "Equity and Justice" and "Trial by Jury," 8″ high, 8½″ wide.

$300

The type of derringer used by John Wilkes Booth to shoot Abraham Lincoln is pictured on the side of this little ceramic cup. The background scene shows Booth leaping onto the stage of the Ford Theater after the assassination. The cup is 3″ high.

$20

Abraham Lincoln was in office and looking weary from the stress of the Civil War when this ceramic mug bearing his likeness was manufactured. It is labeled "President Abraham Lincoln." The same transfer image of Lincoln can be found on an ABC plate. In reasonably good condition, these are scarce relics of a great president. The mug is 3¼″ high.

$475

After the assassination of Abraham Lincoln, a pattern glass was produced that now is known as "Lincoln Drape." This is a goblet showing the Lincoln Drape with tassel. Goblets were also made without the tassel. Glass historians have attributed this pattern to Sandwich, Massachusetts, with the possibility that it was made elsewhere, too. Good quality lead glass, first produced around 1866. Height, 6″.

$95

Many mourning ribbons were made at the time of Lincoln's assassination. This one shows the years that he was in the White House. Length, 3″.

$70

The advanced collector often assembles his collection in frames for easy viewing and display. This outstanding exhibit showing medals, tokens, ferrotypes, and ribbons is from the campaign of 1860 when Abraham Lincoln was elected. Such a collection is not only impressive because of its historic beauty, but is worth thousands of dollars.

A tin collar box made by the Goldsmith & Hoffman Collar Company of New York at the time of the 1876 Centennial pictures the presidential likenesses of Washington and Lincoln, while showing no reference to the incumbent president, Ulysses S. Grant. By 1876 the scandals of the Grant administration had sullied his national reputation.

$65

Andrew Johnson
1865-1869

When he ran for vice-president on the Republican ticket with Abraham Lincoln in 1864, Andrew Johnson's embossed image appeared on medalets, such as this one. Fate intervened, however, and Johnson served little more than a month as vice-president before moving into the office of the presidency following the death of Abraham Lincoln on April 15, 1865.

$40

President Andrew Johnson worked as a tailor before rising to elected office and finally the presidency. His former occupation is emphasized in this United States presidents card measuring 3¾″ × 2½″.

$1

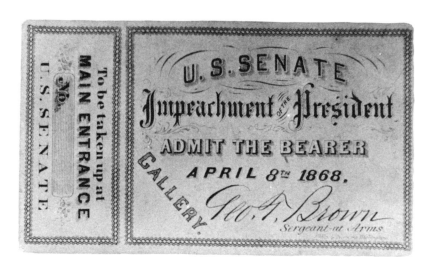

Impeachment tickets for the trial of President Andrew Johnson today have become collectibles. The trial began in March of 1868 and ended on May 16 of that year with Johnson's acquittal. After his term as president, Johnson twice was an unsuccessful candidate for Congress but was elected to the United States Senate in 1874. He served in the Senate until his death on July 31, 1875.

$95

Ulysses S. Grant
1869-1877

Ferrotypes from the 1872 campaign in which Ulysses S. Grant defeated Horace Greeley are shown in this lineup. At left is a jugate showing Grant and his running mate, Henry Wilson. Grant appears alone in the oval tintype in the center. At right is Greeley along with his vice-presidential candidate, Benjamin Brown. All of these are highly desirable items.

Grant-Wilson	**$600**
Grant	**$185**
Greeley-Brown	**$900**

Ulysses S. Grant, looking trim and handsome in his general's uniform, is shown here in the form of a hard-paste Parian bust that perhaps served as a campaign item. Careful attention has been paid to Grant's hair and features in this excellent presidential artifact. The bust stands 7″ high and carries the identification "U.S. GRANT" on the base.

$90

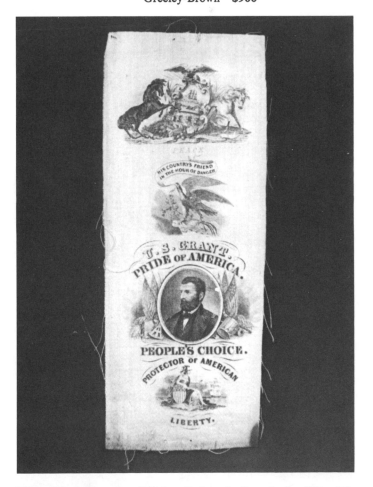

They called him the "Pride of America" and the "People's Choice" in this ribbon turned out for Ulysses S. Grant. An interesting design, 7¾″ long.

$110

51

"Let Us Have Peace" was the slogan for the Ulysses S. Grant-Schuyler Colfax team in the 1860 election. This paper ballot, which also pictures two handicapped veterans from the Civil War, lists other candidates in a hard-to-read, but imaginative manner. 7¾″ × 4″.

$28

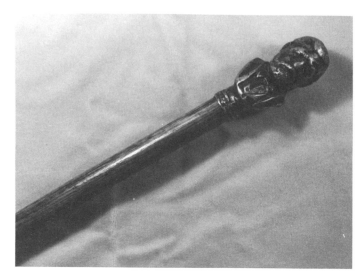

A cane that honors the memory of Grant makes an appropriate addition to any collection of presidential mementos. This one shows the old Civil War hero wearing a somewhat troubled expression, and it bears some of the scars of long usage. The metal cane head is 2⅝″ high.

$95

Ulysses S. Grant's intaglio image appears on the bottom of this glass tumbler along with his campaign slogan, "Let Us Have Peace." The tumbler stands 3½″ high and is a worthy addition for collectors who like to find United States presidents in glass.

$45

Ulysses S. Grant's scandal-plagued administration prompted the creation of this "Tammany Bank," patented in 1873. You put a coin in the upright hand of the Tammany politician and he quickly dumps it into his pocket. It should be noted, too, that a larger coin, such as a quarter, gets into the pocket faster than a penny. The bank is 5¾″ high.

$150

The pictures of eighteen presidents up to and including Ulysses S. Grant appear on this attractively designed engraving of the Dwight Company, made by the American Bank Note Company of New York. The border also honors thirty-eight states. Turned out at the time of the Centennial, the engraving carries the 1776-1876 dates. It measures 9½″ × 8½″.

$60

Ferrotypes and medalets ranging in time from the presidency of Andrew Jackson to Ulysses S. Grant show the interesting qualities of these early mementos. Many collectors specialize in such items. The ferrotypes in the top row include, left to right, Abraham Lincoln, Stephen Douglas, General McClellan, and Grant. The general price category of the items shown would be anywhere from a low of perhaps $40 to a high of $275.

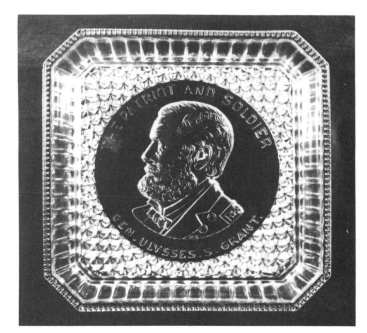

Marketed as a memorial to Ulysses S. Grant, this good-looking glass bread tray was made by Bryce, Higbee & Company, Pittsburgh, in 1885. The intaglio image of Grant, wearing his Civil War uniform, is centered amid a pattern design background. The plate is inscribed, "The Patriot and Soldier." Still available and reasonably priced. The plate measures 9½″ square, with the raised sides 1½″ high.

$30

Wearing his Civil War uniform, Ulysses S. Grant is honored in this modern iron bank. While Grant had his problems as president, his stature as a military leader has remained strong in American history. Although it isn't old, the Grant bank merits a place in a presidential collection. Height, 5½″.

$18

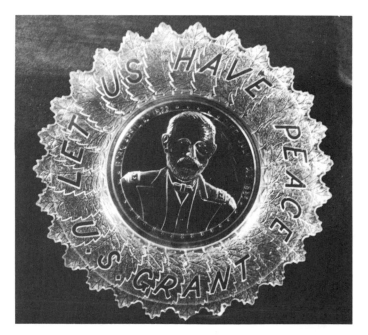

Ulysses S. Grant's home in Galena, Illinois, is shown on this souvenir china sugar holder. The house and surrounding trees are in good color. The piece was made in Dresden and distributed in the United States by Wheelock & Company. This and other souvenir items were sold from the Old Grant Leather Store in Galena. Height, 3½″.

$22

Produced in several colors and in clear glass, the "Let Us Have Peace" plate is a memorial to Ulysses S. Grant and was manufactured shortly after he died in 1885. The center portrait pictures Grant in his general's uniform and the wording gives the date of his birth and death. The border decoration features overlapping maple leaves. The plates are believed to have been made by more than one company. Diameter, 10⅜″.

Color **$55**
Clear **$45**

Rutherford B. Hayes
1877-1881

Voters supported their candidates by wearing brass shells and other decorative portrait framings for the election of 1876, when Rutherford Hayes and Samuel Tilden were the opponents. Shown in this series are, left to right, Hayes and William Wheeler, Hayes, Tilden and Thomas Hendricks, and Tilden.

Hayes-Wheeler	**$250**
Hayes	**$160**
Tilden-Hendricks	**$225**
Tilden	**$150**

Both the presidential and Centennial themes are featured on this Republican ballot turned out on behalf of Republican candidates Rutherford Hayes and William Wheeler.

$40

The Hayes-Wheeler team sought the support of "The Boys in Blue" with this 1876 campaign ribbon. Uncluttered and attractive in its design, the ribbon is 5¼" long.

$125

Backers of Tilden and Hendricks wore this ribbon proudly during the controversial election of 1876. Brightly decorated with the American eagle, stars, stripes, and the jugate likeness of the Democratic candidates, 4½" ribbon makes a fine campaign souvenir.

$150

This miniature Liberty Bell mug was made by the Adams Glass Company of Pittsburgh during the presidential election year of 1876, when the nation also celebrated its centennial. Faintly embossed on the sides of the bell, and almost impossible to see, even when you hold the mug in your hands, are the names "Hayes" and "Wheeler." Also dated "1776-1876." A scarce campaign item. Height, 2″.

$85

The bas-relief features of Rutherford Hayes are pictured on this bronze presidential medal. The base of the bust carries the name "Morgan," and the reverse side shows the March 5, 1877, date on which Hayes was inaugurated. A well-designed medal, with a diameter of 3″.

$35

Not much attention is paid to good detail, but President Rutherford Hayes is among the presidents found in these collectible miniature tobies. Impressed on the back are the dates "1877-1881," the years that Hayes was in office. Above the dates the number "19" is circled. This item is hard to find.

$50

Rutherford B. Hayes is showcased in a little cigar band dish of the kind that was common earlier in this century. The picture is in rich color. Daniel Webster is shown on one of the cigar bands fanning out from the center. Diameter, 5″.

$10

James A. Garfield
1881

The **facsimile** signature of James A. Garfield identifies the presidential candidate on this ironstone plate made for the 1880 election. The transfer image of Garfield is dark and clear. A gold border decorates the rim. Diameter, 8".

$48

Single-picture ribbons were made for the candidates in both major parties for the 1880 campaign. This one pictures the winner, Garfield.

$80

The **Garfield-Arthur** glass campaign mug pictured here is an outstanding example of presidential Americana. Just 2⅛" high, it shows James Garfield on one side and, on the other side is a fine likeness of a politically symbolic raccoon that appears to be thumbing its nose at the opposition. The handle is embossed on one side with the name "Garfield," and misspelled on the other side is the name of his running mate, "Arthur*s*." At the top of the handle is the date 1880. The maker is identified on the base as "Adams & Co. Glass Mfgrs." of Pittsburgh.

$125

Clothing buttons from the 1880 campaign between James Garfield and Winfield Hancock make sturdy campaign souvenirs for the collector. These brass buttons urge support for "Garfield and Arthur" and "Hancock and English." Each measures ¾" in diameter.

Each **$18**

57

William S. Hancock was the Democratic candidate who opposed James A. Garfield in the 1880 presidential campaign. It was a close race and Hancock, a general who distinguished himself during the Civil War, was narrowly defeated. The ironstone plate showing his likeness was made for the campaign. It has a diameter of 7¾″.

$45

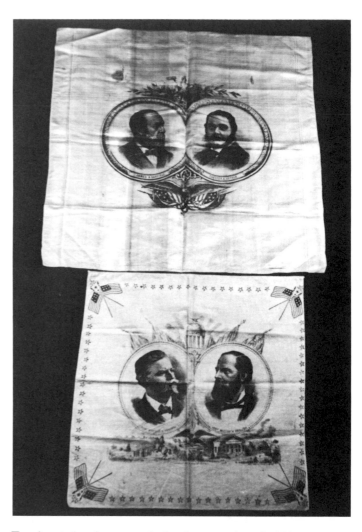

Two jugate bandannas made for the campaign of 1880 manage to combine appropriate flag-waving with the desired political message. The top bandanna shows James Garfield and his running mate, Chester Arthur. The more ornate textile at the bottom pictures Winfield S. Hancock and his vice-presidential candidate, William H. English. Fine campaign items.

Garfield-Arthur **$100**
Hancock-English **$120**

Collar boxes were popular back in 1880, when James Garfield ran for president. This one was made with his finely executed bas-relief likeness on the cover. The wooden boxes are 4¼″ square and 3″ deep. The bottom of this one also bears the license stamp of "The Standard Collar Company," originally licensed under a patent in October of 1872. Garfield's vice-presidential mate, Chester Arthur, is shown on a companion box.

$120

Possibly a campaign item, this nicely decorated glass plate features a fine intaglio image of James A. Garfield and a border that has thirteen stars, two flags, and a shield. The Garfield likeness is acid-etched. The plate appears to have been made by the Crystal Glass Company of Bridgeport, Ohio. Still available, the plates are reasonably priced for their age and quality. Diameter, 6".

$25

This Garfield piece has been called at various times a cup plate or an ashtray. It is the author's view that it more likely is a little pin tray. Made of thick, sturdy glass, the 3" tray has an excellent intaglio image of Garfield and makes a fine presidential glass collectible. Probably a campaign item, with the Crystal Glass Company of Bridgeport, Ohio, believed to be the manufacturer. Hard to find.

$45

James A. Garfield, our second president to be assassinated, is remembered by this Bennington-type pitcher. His embossed image is surrounded by an ornate leafy border, with decorative trim also around the top, bottom, and on the handle. Probably manufactured in 1881 as a memorial piece. Not easily found, the pitcher stands 7½" high.

$200

After Garfield's death, the Adams Glass Company of Pittsburgh changed the mold of its Garfield-Arthur campaign mug to make it a memorial item. The raccoon was removed from one side and replaced by birth and death dates surrounded by a mourning drape. Garfield's image remains on the other side, but the names of Garfield and Arthur have been removed from the handle. Overlooked, however, was the fact that the top of the handle still carried the "1880" campaign mug date—even though the memorial mug was made for the market after Garfield's death in 1881. A fine presidential memento. Height, 2⅛".

$80

Called the martyrs' mug, the bas-relief images of both Abraham Lincoln and James Garfield appear on the sides of this historic glass memento. The dates of their births and assassinations also are shown, and the wreathlike handle is decorated with stars. Made after the death of Garfield by the Adams Glass Company of Pittsburgh. Height, 2½″. In the author's view, this unusual piece has remained a bargain.

$55

Garfield's portrait surrounded by a wreath in the base of this tumbler presumably makes it a memorial item turned out after his assassination in 1881. Height, 3½″.

$40

A large commemorative glass plate was made in the Garfield Drape pattern after the death of President Garfield. The fallen president is framed by the words, "We Mourn Our Nation's Loss" set against a stippled background. The dates that Garfield was born, shot, and died are on the plate, along with stars and floral decorations. Attributed to Adams Glass Company, Pittsburgh. Diameter, 11⅜″.

$55

Known by two names, the "In Remembrance" and "Three Presidents" tray, this heavy glass platter makes a worthy addition to any presidential collection. The central theme features the framed portraits of Washington, Lincoln, and Garfield. The tray was made after the assassination of Garfield, and has a stippled laurel wreath border. It's a good historial piece and appropriate for anyone hunting for memorabilia of our presidents. Length, 12½″.

$55

This memorial plate honors the memory of President James Garfield who died September 19, 1881, after having been shot on July 2, 1881, by Charles Guiteau, who had been seeking a government appointment. The plate has a stippled border, with Garfield's image surrounded by a laurel wreath design and the single word "Memorial." Made by the Adams Glass Company, Pittsburgh.

$35

The oval-framed photographic likeness of President James Garfield is clearly pictured on this rare pink lustre vase. It is the only one that the author has ever seen. The owner of the vase, a political collector of many years, says he is aware of just one other like it. Gracefully designed, it is trimmed with gold and stands 9″ high.

$1,200

A plaster bust, 12″ in height, was made as a memorial to James Garfield after his assassination. His name is impressed into the back. Scrawled in pencil on the back by some long ago owner is the September 19, 1881, date of Garfield's death, along with the mournful comment, "A noble hero." Personal notes of this kind on old presidential collectibles sometimes provide added historic perspective.

$45

The Garfield monument, completed in 1890, is shown in this opaque white plate which honors the memory of James A. Garfield, one of our assassinated presidents. Funds were raised for the monument after Garfield's death in 1881. The monument is located in Cleveland. The plate is believed made by the Westmoreland Specialty Company, Grapeville, Pennsylvania. Diameter, 7½″.

$35

Beautifully decorated, this creamware Garfield memorial pitcher was made by Wedgwood and carries the date of his birth and the year that he took office—and was assassinated. The pitcher is getting harder to find, and because of the quality as well as the design commands a good price.

$600

Chester A. Arthur
1881-1885

Chester A. Arthur left comparatively few collectibles, since he was not nominated by the Republicans in 1884 after having served as president following the assassination of President James Garfield. This collar box was made for the 1880 campaign when he ran with Garfield. It is 4¾″ square and 3″ deep.

$120

He didn't know it when this plate was made, but Chester A. Arthur was destined to be president. The ironstone plate, with a diameter of 8″, pictures him "For Vice-President." An assassin's bullet put him into office for most of what would have been the term of James A. Garfield. The plate has black trim on the rim.

$48

Grover Cleveland
1885-1889
1893-1897

Made for the 1884 campaign, this jugate glass tray pictures the Democratic candidates, Grover Cleveland and Thomas Hendricks. It is an example of the great designs of P.J. Jacobus, who free-lanced his talents, but is most closely identified with the Gillinder & Sons glassworks of Philadelphia. The names of the candidates appear on their images, which are frosted. The border of this handled tray is decorated with a stippled leaf design. The tray is 11½″ wide, 8½″ high.

$210

The 1884 campaign between Grover Cleveland and James G. Blaine may have been politically "dirty," but it nevertheless produced many first-rate collectibles. Included are these two well-made metal pins worn by those who supported the candidates. Each is 2¾″ long.

Each   **$22**

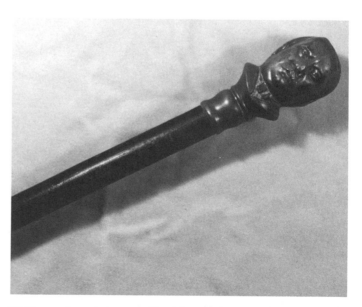

Well-worn from long use, this old campaign cane handle is made in the image of Grover Cleveland. The metal cane head is 3¼″ high.

$90

Something different in the way of presidential collectibles is this framed paper bookplate from a Civil War general, Edward S. Bragg. The brave little Iron Brigade hero, who also served in Congress, delivered a now familiar epigram when he nominated Grover Cleveland at the 1884 convention and challenged Tammany in the process. "They love him, gentlemen," he declared, "and they respect him, not only for himself, for his character, for his integrity and judgment and iron will, but they love him most for the enemies he has made." Bragg himself received party votes for the presidential nomination in 1896. The bookplate is 3″ x 4¼″.

$15

Jugate ribbons made for the 1884 election show Cleveland and Hendricks on the left and Blaine and Logan on the right. Collectors like to find similar items supporting the candidates of the major parties.

Each **$95**

John A. Logan, who went down to defeat as the vice-presidential candidate with James G. Blaine in 1884, is pictured on this unusual metal canteen. Logan, who also is credited as the founder of Memorial Day, was a leader in the Grand Army of the Republic. The canteen, which has an attached chain for carrying, perhaps was manufactured to help whip up political support among his old Civil War buddies. Above Logan's transfer picture is the slogan, "We drank from the same canteen." From spout to bottom, the canteen measures 5¼″. A scarce item.

$150

An ironstone plate with a worn gold border shows James G. Blaine at the time he ran for the presidency in 1884. It was a dirty campaign, and Blaine's loss was attributed in part to an anti-Catholic slur made by one of his backers. A good old campaign souvenir, the plate has a diameter of 8″.

$38

The four Classic Pattern portrait plates designed for the 1884 presidential campaign rank as historic glass artistry at its finest (see page 24). This one pictures Grover Cleveland and is characterized, as are all the plates, by great emphasis on lifelike detail. The plates are hard to find and rank as the best ever produced in the political glass category. Diameter, 11½″.

$225

A companion plate to the one picturing James G. Blaine during his 1884 campaign for the presidency shows John A. Logan, who ran with Blaine as the candidate for vice-president. Logan organized the GAR and also served on the impeachment committee at the time that Andrew Johnson was president. The diameter of the plate measures 8″.

$38

Signed by P.J. Jacobus, the gifted moldmaker who fashioned the four Classic Pattern political plates, this one features the likeness of Thomas Hendricks, the running mate of Cleveland in the 1884 campaign. The signature of Jacobus is found at the lower edge of Hendricks' right shoulder. The two other Classic plates that were made showed similar acid-finish portraits of James Blaine and John Logan. In all, the glassmaking quality is unexcelled. Diameter, 11½″.

$230

There were many china plates circulated in 1884 to help the election chances of James G. Blaine, and this navy blue portrait campaign item was one of them. The border also is trimmed in blue. Diameter, 8″.

$38

Made by Johnson Brothers, England, this Cleveland plate was produced as one of a campaign set for the election of 1884. Good quality ironstone. The other plate pictures Cleveland's vice-presidential candidate, Thomas Hendricks. Diameter, 8½″.

$48

Thomas Hendricks, who ran with Cleveland in 1884, was installed as vice-president in March of 1885, but died in November of that same year. This plate was made as one of a pair for the Democratic candidates. Royal Ironstone China, made by Johnson Brothers, England. Diameter, 8½″.

$42

Well-defined facial features and darker hair make this Grover Cleveland plate a little different than some of the others. Probably manufactured for the campaign of 1884. Diameter, 8″.

$42

Grover Cleveland's portrait is pressed into the bottom of this clear glass tumbler. Probably a campaign item from 1884. Height, 3½".

$45

Made for the 1884 campaign, this 6″ ironstone creamer shows a familiar portrait of Cleveland, with Hendricks, his running mate, on the other side.

$80

Grover Cleveland's years as president are recalled in this excellently detailed plaster bust, made for use as a paperweight or to hang on a wall. Probably made during his first term in office from 1884-1888. Height, 6″.

$18

The 1884 campaign of Grover Cleveland and Thomas Hendricks is remembered by this star-decorated old "C & H" belt buckle. Length 3¼″, width, 2¼″.

$22

Metal-framed cardboard portraits of the candidates were turned out for the 1884 election, along with brass clothing buttons. Cleveland is shown at the left and Blaine on the right. The top button urges support for Blaine-Logan and the other has the embossed names of Cleveland-Hendricks.

Cleveland	**$65**
Blaine	**$50**
Blaine-Logan	**$25**
Cleveland-Hendricks	**$22**

Brooms and a rooster decorate this interesting 1888 campaign scarf made to promote "Our Candidates," Grover Cleveland and Allen Thurman. The scarf is 18½″ square.

$100

This heavy ironstone compote is from the unsuccessful campaign of Grover Cleveland, seeking a second term in 1888. Cleveland and his Democratic vice-presidential candidate, Allen Thurman, are pictured in reddish-brown transfer images inside the bowl. An unusual jugate piece of presidential campaign china. The bowl has a diameter of 8¾″, and the compote stands 4¾″ high.

$190

A **good transfer** likeness of Grover Cleveland appears on this ironstone mug made by G.M. & Son of East Liverpool, Ohio. An unusual item, 5½″ tall.

$70

Finding one of these delicate kerosene lamp chimneys from a presidential race poses a real challenge for the collector. This beauty shows Allen Thurman set against a flag-decorated frosted glass background, with a similar portrait of Cleveland on the other side. Thurman was Cleveland's vice-presidential partner in the 1888 election. The chimney is 8″ high.

$300

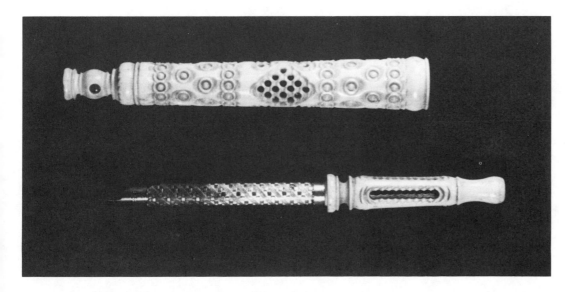

Even stanhopes played a role in popularizing our American presidents. This one also served as a pen. When not in use, the pen was inserted into the ivory holder, and the owner could enjoy the thrill of looking through that little hole near the end and seeing—lo and behold—"President Cleveland." When closed, the pen is 5½″ long. Little metal pig stanhopes also were used for less flattering political purposes.

$70

Encircled in the base of this unusual round paperweight is the picture of Grover Cleveland. The weight probably was made for Cleveland's 1892 bid for the presidency, when he defeated Benjamin Harrison. Diameter, 3″.

$65

In 1892, when Grover Cleveland was elected to a second nonconsecutive term in the White House, he ran with Adlai E. Stevenson, whose grandson would be a candidate for president sixty years later. This jugate ribbon, bright with color, is from the 1892 campaign. Length, 6¼″.

$90

Grover Cleveland and his 1892 vice-presidential candidate Adlai Stevenson are pictured on opposite sides of this clever brass pillbox. The box is shaped like four stacked coins and bears the 1892 date along with the inscription, "My Stack on Cleveland." A similar pillbox was made for Benjamin Harrison and Whitelaw Reid. Good addition to any political collection.

$45

Grover Cleveland had just taken office for his second nonconsecutive term as president when this metal bust was made for national distribution. It was well done and an excellent likeness. Cleveland's name is on the front of the bust and an 1893 copyright date is on the back. It stands 8½″ tall.

$48

Benjamin Harrison
1889-1893

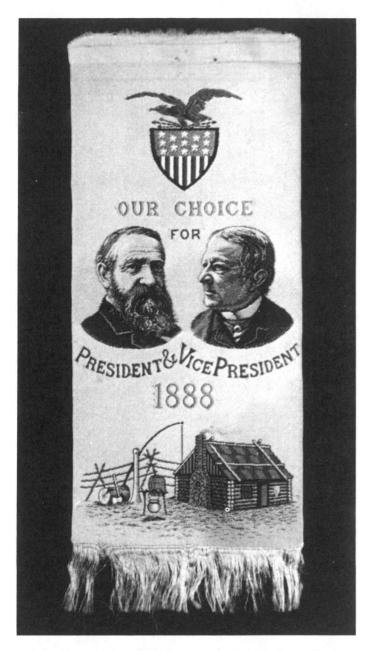

A **campaign egg** for 1888 shows a gold-plated tin rooster crowing for Harrison and Morton. Made of wood, these eggs operated by way of an inner spring arrangement that made the rooster pop up with its political message. Many were given away by merchants as sales gimmicks in 1888, and few are found in perfect working order, yet they're excellent souvenirs of the old presidential campaign process. With the rooster crowing, they measure 3½″ high.
$210

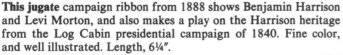

This jugate campaign ribbon from 1888 shows Benjamin Harrison and Levi Morton, and also makes a play on the Harrison heritage from the Log Cabin presidential campaign of 1840. Fine color, and well illustrated. Length, 6¼″.
$90

Made to look like Benjamin Harrison, this metal match holder was patented in time to be used in the campaign of 1888. The latch opens at the base, and there's a rough surface for match-scratching on the bottom. A fine presidential item, 2¾″ high.
$120

Benjamin Harrison and Levi Morton are shown in this coveted jugate glass tray designed by P.J. Jacobus for the 1888 campaign. A similar tray also was made for Cleveland and Thurman. The same stippled-leaf borders used on trays made for the 1884 campaign were used in 1888, although on the later trays there are no handles. The portraits of the candidates are frosted. The tray is 9½″ wide, 8½″ high.

$200

Benjamin Harrison appears on this ironstone plate, probably made for his campaign in 1888 against Grover Cleveland. The transfer print shows the sketched image of Harrison, and the plate has gold trim on the inner and outside border of the rim. Diameter, 8″.

$48

Benjamin Harrison is the presidential subject of this hard-to-find old tile made by C. Pardee Works, Perth Amboy, New Jersey. Harrison's well defined, embossed likeness on the purplish brown tile is enhanced by a heavy glaze. The tile is 6″ x 6″ and sought after by political collectors.

$65

A seldom-seen trivet featuring the center image of Benjamin Harrison framed by a horseshoe may have been a campaign item in 1888. Ferrotypes with Harrison inside a brightly colored enameled horseshoe pin inscribed with the words "Luck" and "Victory" were made for the 1888 race. The Harrison trivet is 5″ long.

$75

Sun-faded pictures of Benjamin Harrison and Levi Morton, plus a hand-printed slogan, "Harrison and Morton and Protection to American Industries" show this to be an old homemade jugate paperweight. Scrawled in well worn pencil writing on the base is this personal message, "Nov. 2, 1888. Harrison will carry N. York by 40,000 and Ind. by 6,000, and he will take his seat and don't you forget it. G. E. Davis." That's what you call real political fervor. Size, 4″ x 2⅝″.

$75

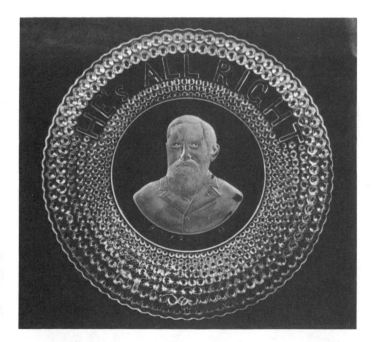

In a familiar political rally chant the crowd would shout, "What's the matter with Harrison?" And in a roar would come the reply, "He's all right!" That kind of noisy performance led to the design of this delightful and rare platter, made for Harrison's campaign against Grover Cleveland. The hobnail border, lettering, and the centering of the candidate's portrait is like the "Reform" plate made for Cleveland. Harrison's image is frosted. It is the author's view that this plate, which has a diameter of 10″, was made by Bryce, Higbee & Company of Pittsburgh.

$190

Stars decorate this old campaign torch which was used to enliven political gatherings as voters whooped it up for their favorite candidate. There are many varieties of torches and some collectors specialize in that field. Prices vary, with rarities justifiably expensive.

$45

Even dogs and cats got into the act when Grover Cleveland and Benjamin Harrison were presidential opponents. The hard-to-find milk glass plate pictured shows a dog and two cats above the slogan "He's All Right." Generally, that slogan was applied to Harrison, who won the 1888 election, but lost in 1892. Diameter, 6¼".

$85

A glass campaign hat made for Benjamin Harrison's second race against Grover Cleveland in 1892 plays upon the memories of his grandfather, President Willliam H. Harrison. The 2¼″ hat bears the slogans, "The Same Old Hat" and "He's All Right." They were made in clear and milk glass, and were manufactured by the United States Glass Company.

$60

"One good term deserves another" says the slogan above "the Harrison hat" pictured on the base of this domed 1892 campaign paperweight. It was made to promote a second term for Benjamin Harrison, with Whitelaw Reid as his vice-presidential nominee. It's marked "Harrison & Reid" and also carries the Latin inscription, "In hoc signo vinces," which translates to something like, "By this sign we shall win." (They lost.) Diameter, 3″.

$95

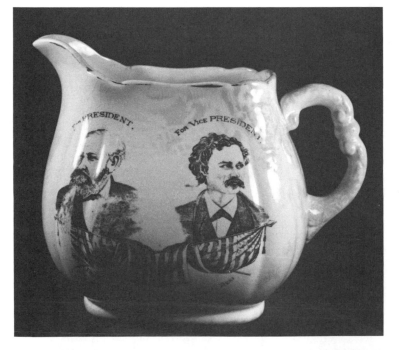

Benjamin Harrison, seeking reelection to a second term, had Whitelaw Reid as his running mate in the 1892 election. Both are shown on this Dresden china campaign pitcher, with their transfer images appearing on both sides. Collectors seek jugate items, so this scarce 6½″ pitcher goes fast when it occasionally appears on the market.

$190

Another well-made ribbon from the last quarter of the nineteenth century picturing Benjamin Harrison and Whitelaw Reid, was produced for the GOP losers in the 1892 presidential election. In bright red, white, and blue colors, the ribbon is 6¼″ long.

$85

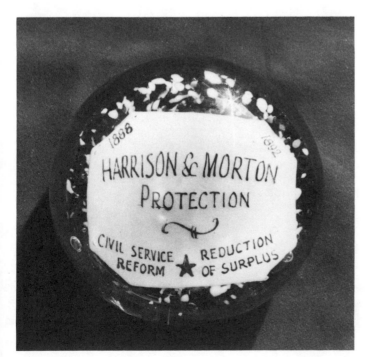

Sought after by historical glass collectors as well as those who pursue presidential Americana is this frosted glass statuette of Benjamin Harrison. Probably made for his 1888 campaign, the statuette stands 5¾″ high and, as this photo shows, is well designed. Of added interest is the fact that it was produced to fit atop a tall, black amethyst fluted pedestal bottle. Even without the base, which adds about $125 more to the price, the statuette is an impressive and scarce souvenir of Harrison's presidency.

$165

Bearing the slogan that appears on an old campaign textile, this large "Harrison & Morton" paperweight really may have had nothing to do with the presidential campaign. While it makes an excellent presidential novelty, and has genuine value as a paperweight, it lacks historic integrity. The author has seen, for example, a weight made exactly the same way—only featuring Mickey Mouse! Diameter, 4½″.

$100

William McKinley
1897-1901

The designer of this 1896 campaign paperweight put his own name on it, lower center, along with the date. He called William McKinley "A winner," and mentioned the McKinley slogan of "Protection" and "Prosperity," while placing the words "Sound Money" above the head of vice-presidential nominee Garret Hobart. The designer goofed, however, by misspelling McKinley as "McKinlly." An amusing memento, 4″ long, 2½″ wide.

$45

Matching hatpins were made for William McKinley and his frail wife, Ida, for the campaign of 1896. The "Protection" slogan is on the McKinley hatpin, while the one showing Mrs. McKinley is brightly adorned with a colored ribbon. Each pin is 6″ long.

Each **$22**

A jugate plate made for the 1896 campaign shows photographic transfers of the winners, William McKinley and Garret Hobart. Marked on the back is "Semi-Vitreous" beneath a crown-topped trademark. Diameter, 9″.

$45

Little lacy portrait plates with a forget-me-not border were manufactured for the 1896 campaign between William McKinley and William Jennings Bryan. On this one, a sober-faced McKinley is etched into the base. Made by the United States Glass Company, the plates have a diameter of 5¼″.

$35

A rare cast-iron clock advocating the candidacy of William McKinley in the 1896 campaign features a dial made in the shape of a coin that reads, "Sound Money," and carries the date 1896. Topped by a bust of McKinley, the clock also is decorated with symbols of commerce in line with the McKinley slogan of "Protection-Prosperity." An exceptional item, 14½″ high.

$750

The full dinner pail was one of the symbols used by the political forces of William McKinley in the 1896 campaign against William Jennings Bryan. Cleverly made with a wire handle and a metal cup for a top, the pail is 4¼″ high from the spout to the base. A fine campaign artifact, and difficult to find.

$190

A jugate paperweight pictures the 1896 vice-presidential candidate, Garret Hobart, on the left and presidential candidate William McKinley on the right. Usually the candidates are shown the other way around. An interesting campaign weight, 4″ x 2½″.

$38

Probably made for the 1896 campaign, this plate pictures a rather grim looking William McKinley along with his slogan, "Patriotism, Protection, Prosperity." The reverse side is marked "E. L. P. Co., Waco, china." Diameter, 9″.

$30

Whistle-stopping gained acceptance as an effective campaigning technique in 1896, when William Jennings Bryan spoke to audiences in many small communities. This illustrated paper schedule of his "Special Train" covered only one day, October 30, 1896, and on that day he stopped in fifteen communities in Wisconsin. The itinerary noted that Bryan would "speak from the rear end of his car." Size, 5¾″ x 3½″.

$5

"Protection and Plenty" is the McKinley campaign slogan surrounding his image that is impressed in the bottom of this clear glass tumbler. Made for the 1896 campaign by McKee & Brothers of Pittsburgh. Height, 3¾″.

$45

This campaign tumbler portrays a steady-eyed William McKinley under the heading, "Our Next President," which was made for the campaign of 1896. Etched on the back of the 3½″ blown tumbler in large letters is "Emma, 1896." At this stage in history, it seems rather nice to know that Emma's man won.

$48

78

A rare black amethyst glass ribbon plate with the bas-relief image of William Jennings Bryan made for the 1896 presidential campaign is a highly desirable political collectible. On some of the plates, Bryan's image may be found painted silver, just as the face of William McKinley on the milk-white Gothic border plates often is found painted gold. The ribbon in the border of the plate shown here is silver, an appropriate color for the campaign. Black amethyst plates showing either Bryan or McKinley are extremely hard to find and should be treasured. Diameter, 9".

$200

Among the most attractive political glass pieces ever manufactured is this 9" Gothic border, milk-white ribbon plate picturing William McKinley in bas-relief. The likeness of McKinley appears in gold, and the ribbon decorating the border is gold to emphasize the 1896 gold vs. silver issue. Designed by David Barker, the plates were produced by the Canton Glass Company of Marion, Indiana. Because of their beauty, an impressive number of these plates have survived by being passed along in families.

$125

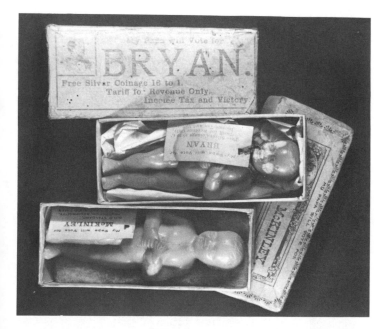

Soap babies were made for the presidential campaign of 1896 between William McKinley and William Jennings Bryan. This was the gold vs. silver campaign, and babies were packaged in boxes that emphasized that political issue. Each baby was tagged with a little card telling why "My Papa will vote for . . ." (either McKinley or Bryan). Finding these soap babies in good condition, particularly without broken feet, is difficult. Each baby is 4¼" long, and the boxes are a main part of their value.

Each **$45**

This heavy metal bust combines the look of antiquity with reasonably accurate facial detail, adding to its appeal as a presidential collectible. Probably made around the time of the 1896 campaign. The front of the base is marked "Wm McKinley" and on the reverse is "G. B. Haines, Chicago." Height, 7″.

$45

A tin horn was blown for "Patriotism, Protection, Prosperity" promised in the 1896 campaign of William McKinley, and it still blows with gusto. The campaign slogan is imprinted in the tin. A good souvenir of the excitement of past campaigns. Height, 4¼″

$50

Another campaign item is this straw hat made of milk glass. The hatband is gold, and pictured inside the hat is the face of William McKinley. Similar hats were made with silver bands and pictured William Jennings Bryan. The hats were made for the 1896 campaign by McKee & Brothers of Pittsburgh and served as handy little pin tray novelties. Unfortunately, not too many survived.

$80

William McKinley looks out soberly from inside this thick paperweight, which probably was circulated for the campaign of 1896. Beneath the picture, in a facsimile of his own writing, is "Yours truly, Wm McKinley." Length 4″, width 2½″.

$42

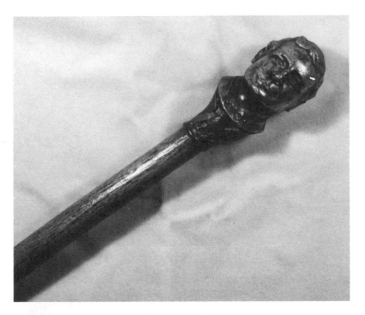

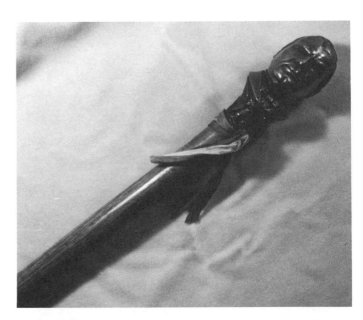

William Jennings Bryan's attempt to win the presidency on the issue of advocating the free coinage of silver is not overlooked in the decoration on this cane head from the 1896 campaign. Well designed and interesting, the metal head is 3½″ long.

$85

William McKinley was calling for protection in 1896 and that's the message on this impressive cane head used by his followers in the campaign against William Jennings Bryan. A fine presidential collectible. The head of the cane measures 3½″.

$85

This McKinley plate, made in 7″ and 9″ sizes, was produced for the 1896 campaign between McKinley and Bryan. Made of sturdy glass, it carries the shielded image of McKinley, his "Protection and Plenty" slogan, and a starred border. Glass researcher and author William Heacock (in the *Antique Trader,* February 7, 1979 issue) stated that the plates were advertised in an 1896 trade publication "prior to the elections." Still offered rather frequently on the market, the rope-edged plates are worthy of any collection of presidential memorabilia.

$35

The McKinley-Bryan battle for the presidency in 1896 is reflected in this well-decorated shot glass advertising Perry Buggies of Indianapolis. The glass, which is 2¾″ high, bears the embossed images of McKinley and Bryan with the words "gold" and "silver" in circles above their heads. The glass also measures up to four tablespoons, and on the opposite side measures liquor in terms of "ladies," "gentlemen" and, for those who demand more, there is a bas-relief likeness of a pig. Beneath the liquor side is the inscription, "Look for the puzzle." An unusual political keepsake and not easy to find.

$65

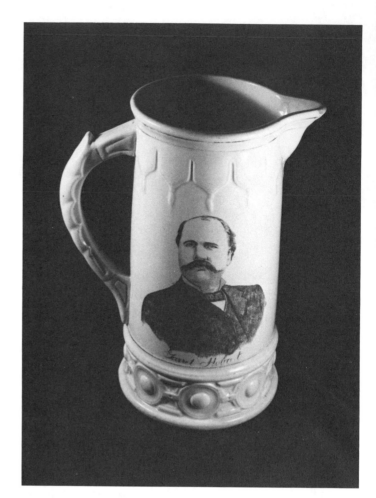

Covered glass mugs, which some believe actually served as mustard jars, were manufactured by the United States Glass Company in 1896 to promote the candidacies of both William McKinley and William Jennings Bryan. Attractively designed with a stipple finish, this one shows "Maj. Wm. McKinley" with the slogan "Protection and Prosperity." Well-molded with stippling and fancy trim, the 3½" mug shown here has the original cover, which adds about $12 to the price. The mugs still appear quite frequently in antique shops, at shows, and in auctions, but prices are rising.

$42

Garret Hobart, the vice-presidential candidate with William McKinley in 1896, is shown on the reverse side of this highly prized 10" campaign pitcher that features McKinley's likeness on the other side. Hobart died on November 21, 1899, and the office was not filled until the election of 1900. This is a superior campaign item.

$300

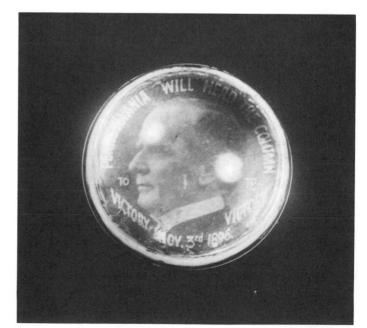

"Pennsylvania will head the column" says this domed paperweight, picturing William McKinley. The insert in the paperweight was made for the 1896 campaign. Diameter, 3".

$32

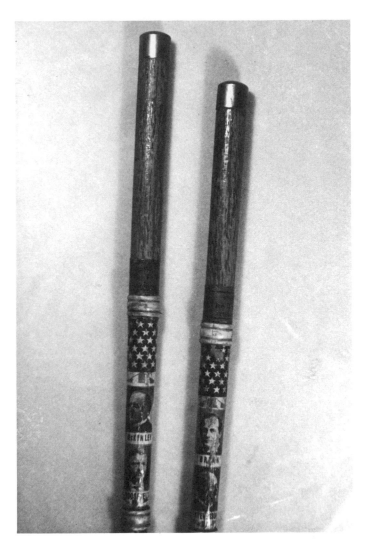

This rare milk-glass jugate campaign plate shows in excellent bas-relief the 1900 presidential election candidates for the Democrats, William Jennings Bryan and Adlai Stevenson. Voters were familiar with both men, since Bryan had lost to McKinley in 1896 and Stevenson had served as vice-president under Grover Cleveland after the election of 1892. The plate is heavy, with a well defined floral leaf border. Attributed by glass historians Regis and Mary Ferson to the Indiana Tumbler and Goblet Company, Greentown, Indiana. Diameter, 8¼″.

$200

Two metal-topped canes showing pictures of the presidential and vice-presidential candidates in the election of 1900 are treasured today by political collectors. The cane on the left shows the McKinley-Roosevelt ticket, while on the right are Bryan and his campaign mate, Stevenson. Interesting jugate souvenirs.

Each **$95**

This McKinley plate was marketed for the 1896 campaign and shows McKinley's signature and the date beneath his portrait. The border is trimmed with fanciful touches of gold, and the transfer portrait is in reddish brown. Diameter, 7½″.

$35

The McKinley-Roosevelt presidential ticket is pictured in a reddish brown transfer on this little milk-white campaign plate with a "one-O-one" border. The rim edging of the plate, manufactured in 1900, is green. Variations of coloring have been found, however, so the collector should not hold back on buying such a plate simply because the decorations are different. Often the images of the candidates are faint. Diameter, 5¼″.

$45

Among the paperweights turned out for President William McKinley was this one made in the form of a seven-pointed star. McKinley's domed picture in the center is surrounded by a beaded ring which some glass historians believe is designed to create an electric lightbulb effect in an era when such lights were still new. The paperweight is 5″ wide.

$50

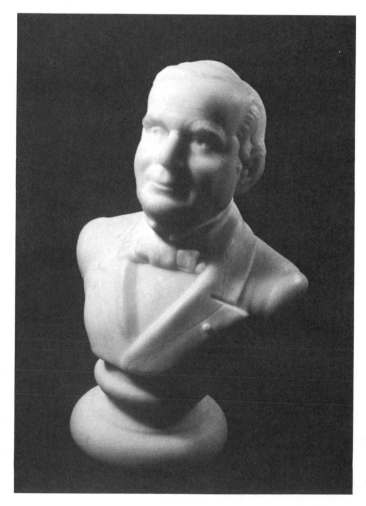

William McKinley is immortalized in this white opaque glass statuette, which was also made in clear glass with a frosted finish. Probably manufactured by the Canton Glass Company or McKee Brothers. McKinley statuettes are scarce in either clear or milk glass and are believed to date from his first term in the White House. The statuettes have moderately well-defined features and are 5¼″ high.

$150

Because of her frail health, President McKinley was extremely thoughtful and considerate of his wife, Ida, pictured on this china plate which was one of a series of six made for the wives of the presidents. They were married in Canton, Ohio, on January 25, 1871. With the oval image of Mrs. McKinley in color, the plate, which bears an Imperial China marking, measures 6″ x 6″.

$12

Richly colored old serving trays such as this one showing McKinley have been passed along in families. Many have holes near the top, from owners who used them as pictures to decorate their walls. An excellent presidential collectible measuring 16″ in length.

$75

All the presidents up through William McKinley appear on this tin serving tray distributed to promote the sale of shoes. The tray is highlighted by beautiful color and presents brief biographical data on all the presidents on the top and bottom rim. More than 17″ long, the tray was made around 1900.

$115

An unusual memento of the presidency of William McKinley is this sturdy, ornate napkin holder. The round focal point frames the celluloid-protected button image of McKinley and can be lifted up on one side for clamplike use as the result of a durable underside spring. The engraved design on the metal ring adds to the attractiveness of this complex little gadget. It also is marked, "Pat. July 1900, J. Frame, Toledo, O." Length, 2¼".

$35

President McKinley is pictured on this interesting cardboard fan which cooled the holder when pressure was applied to the wooden handle, causing the fan to spin one way and then another. The inset shows the Temple of Music at the Pan American Exposition in Buffalo, New York, where the president was shot. Strangely, the other side of the fan, decorated in graceful color, carries the slogan, "Welcome to Our Visitor."

$40

A garland of flowers surrounds William McKinley's likeness on this heavy and somewhat different ceramic plate. Possibly made after McKinley's assassination in 1901. Diameter, 9¼".

$35

The American flag, a star shining down from heaven, a wreath around his head, flowers, and his most memorable last quotation all are used to decorate this memorial jackknife honoring President McKinley. The three-bladed, 2¾" knife was made in Germany for "Our Martyred President." His deathbed quote is on the reverse side.

$38

McKinley's comments about having a little savings bank in the home are quoted on the side of this bank which was distributed by the State Bond and Mortgage Company. McKinley's picture and message appear on cardboard which is framed by the metal edging. Size, 4¼″ x 3¼″.

$45

After McKinley's assassination, this blown glass memorial tumbler appeared on the market. It pictures a view of McKinley facing to his right with the wording, "Our President, 1897 to 1901." Height, 3¾″.

$42

A McKinley memorial bread tray quoting the president's deathbed comments was made after his assassination in 1901. The McKinley figure in the center of the tray closely resembles the McKinley image, with slight variations, that appeared on the gold standard tray made for the campaign of 1896. Birth and death dates have been added, and the tray has a wreath border. Still rather easily found, and often in the bargain category. Probably made by the United States Glass Company. Length, 10½″.

$30

Youth still came through on the face of William Jennings Bryan in this jugate paperweight made for the campaign of 1900. Pictured with Bryan is his running mate, Adlai Stevenson. The heavy rectangular weight is 4¼″ x 3″ in size.

$35

Among the scarce presidential campaign items from William McKinley is this unusual lacy milk glass plate, which features a photograph of McKinley under a round center layer of clear glass. The oval picture is framed with blue paint, which has chipped under the clear glass. The outer rim of the portrait area is decorated with gold. The diameter of the plate, believed made in 1900, is 8¼".

$95

Theodore Roosevelt
1901-1909

Teddy Roosevelt's political star was rising when this Rough Rider clock, showing him in full uniform astride his horse, was patented on April 25, 1899. The following year he was nominated as vice-presidential candidate on the Republican ticket. Before the end of 1901, because of William McKinley's assassination, he had become president. The clock is a Seth Thomas. Height, 10½".

$90

His background as a Rough Rider was exploited to help Theodore Roosevelt rise in politics. Here he's shown, sword raised, thundering along on his horse—presumably up San Juan Hill. The tin serving tray is 16" long.

$100

These ribbons were made for President Theodore Roosevelt's visit to Butte, Montana, in 1903 and were distributed by the Montana Drug Company. The decorations and printing are in color. Length, 6¾″.

$12

Made by Wedgwood, this blue and white Theodore Roosevelt plate with a leafy border carries a reverse-side quote from a speech given by the president in Syracuse, New York, in 1903. Old and desirable, this would be a quality addition for the collector. Diameter, 9″.

$60

Alton Brooks Parker and Henry Gassaway Davis were the Democratic hopefuls in the 1904 Democratic campaign to defeat Theodore Roosevelt and his vice-presidential partner, Charles Warren Fairbanks. The Parker-Davis team is pictured on this jugate paperweight, with the shield and flags in color. Length, 4″, width, 2½″.

$50

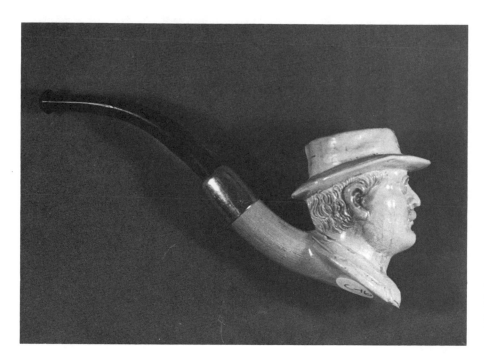

Theodore Roosevelt, garbed in his Rough Rider hat, is shown in this charming figural pipe, probably a campaign item dating from 1904. The pipe is 5¼″ long.

$75

This Teddy Roosevelt watch fob was used during the campaign of 1904 when he ran with Charles Fairbanks. Rather common, size is 1⅜″.

$10

One of the brightest and most unusual glass trays made for the political field is the oval bread tray manufactured by the United States Glass Company for the campaign of 1904. It shows the frosted image of Roosevelt, wearing his pince-nez. The central portrait is surrounded by a delightful border that pictures teddy bears, his Rough Rider paraphernalia, the eagle and shield, and his slogan, "A Square Deal." The slogan is decorated with crossed clubs, presumably to indicate Roosevelt's policy of carrying "a big stick." The edge of the border is made to resemble a twig. Fortunately, these trays, which are 10¼″ long, still come onto the market—but prices are rising.

$125

Americans liked the fact that Teddy Roosevelt spared the life of a little bear on a hunting trip and responded to scores of items that featured the teddy bear theme. This one shows Roosevelt kneeling next to a tree stump, which is being climbed by a bear. It is entitled, "Teddy and the Bear." Made of china, it is 3½" high.

$50

Teddy Roosevelt's teeth inspired the creation of this campaign noisemaker, described by the Chicago manufacturer as "more fun in a minute than a barrel of monkeys." Made of colored metal, the item was actually a horn so political activists could whoop it up for their candidate. Back in Teddy's day, these noisemakers sold for ten cents each. Today they are considerably more valuable.

$75

The Roosevelt bears always seemed to be having a whale of a time when Teddy Roosevelt was in the White House. This little plate with the scalloped border shows the bears engaged in a game of football while, as the verse says, the "dudes remain at home." The transfer is in color. Diameter, 5½".

$48

It takes a steady hand to put the white teeth in Teddy Roosevelt's mouth in this little presidential skill game. The teeth are tiny white balls that roll freely, and it doesn't take much of a wiggle to send them careening in the wrong direction. The face is in color, the rim is metal, and there's a mirror on the reverse side. Made during Roosevelt's years in the White House. Diameter, 2¼".

$125

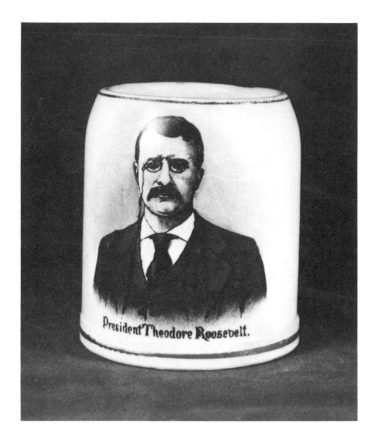

Theodore Roosevelt was in office when this little ceramic mug, showing the president in full color, was made in Germany. Gold striping decorates the top and bottom of the mug, with the country of origin stamped in red on the bottom.

$45

Teddy Roosevelt's likeness impressed in copper with a wooden frame perhaps was made for his Bull Moose campaign in 1912. A similar brass plaque also was produced for Woodrow Wilson. Size, 6½″ x 4¾″.

$35

Highlights in the life of Theodore Roosevelt are dramatized in rim scenes on this popular Rowland & Marsellus Company blue-and-white plate made in Staffordshire, England. Sold at the time that Roosevelt held office, it is one of the basic additions to any presidential collection and still a bargain. Diameter, 10″.

$35

The entire Roosevelt family is identified on this little aluminum pin tray with decorated corners. The group includes, in addition to President Teddy Roosevelt and Mrs. Roosevelt, Archibald, Theodore Jr., Kermit, Alice, Quentin, and Ethel. Size, 6¼″ x 4¼″.

$15

It was Teddy Roosevelt who said that he was throwing his hat in the ring, and some enterprising bandanna-maker went out and produced a campaign textile stressing the message. Roosevelt's hat is shown in a center ring on this red and white bandanna with the initials TR and a caricatured Roosevelt used for decorations. The size is 19¾" x 18".

$42

The Rough Rider image never hurt Theodore Roosevelt at the polls and it's reflected again here in an iron bank. Popular with collectors, the bank is 5" high.

$115

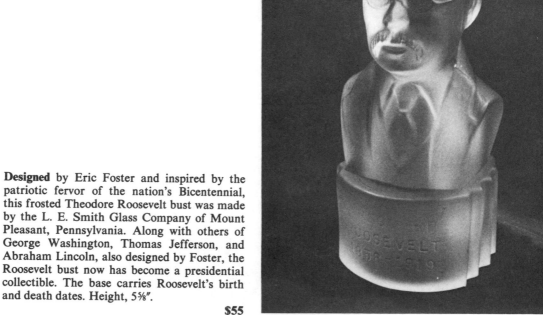

Designed by Eric Foster and inspired by the patriotic fervor of the nation's Bicentennial, this frosted Theodore Roosevelt bust was made by the L. E. Smith Glass Company of Mount Pleasant, Pennsylvania. Along with others of George Washington, Thomas Jefferson, and Abraham Lincoln, also designed by Foster, the Roosevelt bust now has become a presidential collectible. The base carries Roosevelt's birth and death dates. Height, 5⅝".

$55

William Howard Taft
1909-1913

Taft's fat and jovial features are emphasized in the center of this 1908 campaign plate. Made of milk glass and decorated with a patriotic border showing eagles, flags, and stars, the plate became a favorite of those voters who believed that Taft was the right man to succeed Teddy Roosevelt. The diameter of the plate, produced in conjunction with another honoring William Jennings Bryan, is 7¼″.

$60

Bryan's third try for the presidency in 1908 is remembered by this milk glass plate molded in bas-relief, with a similar plate made for the candidacy of William Howard Taft. Flags, stars, and eagles decorate the border. Although they are offered for sale only infrequently, the price on these plates has remained reasonable and they therefore make good additions to either a milk glass or presidential collection. Diameter, 7¼″.

$60

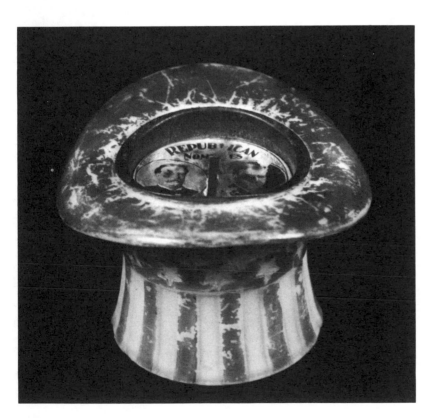

An Uncle Sam hat milk glass bank in red, white, and blue was made for the nominees in the 1908 presidential election. This one features the Republican candidates, William Howard Taft and James S. Sherman. The slotted tin closure on these little banks was topped by paper pictures of the nominees, with some showing just the man running for president. When circulated, the campaign hats were filled with candies. Many of the paper photos were torn when children later used the banks to save pennies. Height, 2½″.

$65

This jugate campaign tumbler shows William H. Taft "For President" and James S. Sherman "For Vice President." Made in 1908 to promote the Republican candidates. Height, 3½".

$48

A twinkle of humor seems to be in the eyes of William Howard Taft in this plate, a companion piece to the Sevres campaign issue that also produced a plate for candidate William Jennings Bryan. The well done transfer image of Taft is reddish brown, and the plate has a gold floral border. Diameter, 8".

$40

"Our choice" campaign plate for 1908 showing William Howard Taft features gold trim on the edge, with "Carrollton China" on the back. Diameter, 8½".

$25

Fine quality Sevres plates were produced for the campaign of 1908. This one shows William Jennings Bryan who at that time was about to suffer his third presidential defeat. This is an excellent likeness of an aging Bryan, with an attractive gold floral border. Diameter, 8".

$38

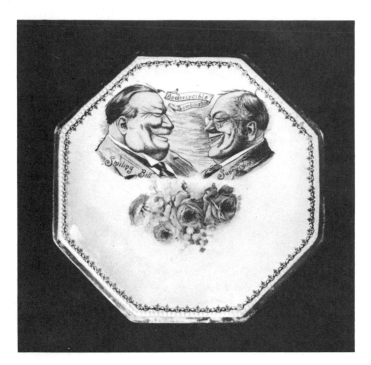

The **"Smiling Bill"** and "Sunny Jim" plates made for the successful candidates in the 1908 election have become popular collectors' items. This octagonal, green and gold-edged plate decorated with flowers shows Taft at the left with Sherman, his vice-president. Both men seem to be enjoying themselves. The little banner between them carries the message, "An Invincible Combination." The plate measures 7″ across.

$60

Taft and Sherman, the Grand Old Party duo in 1908, are shown on this attractive little campaign tin tip tray. Excellent color for the candidates, flags, White House, and trim. The rim of the 4¼″ tray lists all the Republican presidential nominees from 1856 on. Not easily found.

$42

Presidential postcards decorated with cloth were made for the campaign of 1908. Here are two of them, with Teddy Roosevelt doing a selling job for William Howard Taft on the left, and William Jennings Bryan holding a balloon made of cloth while talking to the Democratic donkey on the right. Scarce.

Each   **$50**

This jugate plate, showing William Howard Taft and James S. Sherman, was a Staffordshire product imported by the Rowland & Marsellus Company of New York. Shown around the rim are key Washington, D.C., buildings, Mount Vernon and the Washington Monument. A fine blue-and-white plate of historic significance. Diameter, 10″.

$48

One of Taft's nicknames was "Billy Possum," so of course there were cartoons, postcards, and other items linking him to that identification. This scarce little metal child's mug, with silverplate all worn off, shows Billy Possum wearing a cap and carrying a set of golf clubs, since Taft enjoyed golf for his much-needed exercise. The bottom marking shows this to be quadruple plate of the Eureka Silver Company, U.S.A. Height, 2½″.

$95

Scarce political glass bread trays were made for the Republican and Democratic candidates for the election of 1908. This one pictures the Republicans, William Howard Taft and J.S. Sherman, along with the GOP elephant and the American eagle on a shield. Taft and Sherman are described as "Our Candidates" on most of these trays, but this one says "Our Presidents," indicating that the mold was changed after their election. An excellent presidential memento, more than 11″ long.

$150

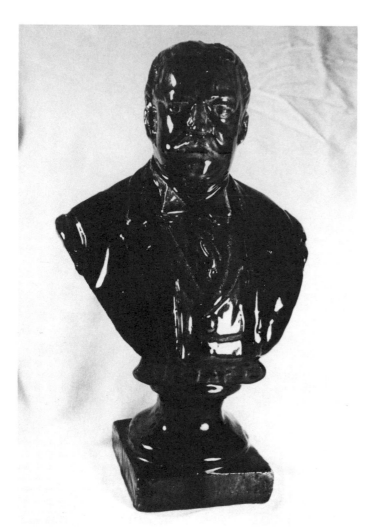

William Howard Taft, looking dapper with a handlebar mustache, is glorified in this fancy-stemmed pipe made by Gambier of Paris. Taft is identified by his name on one side of the pipe. The facial features, hair, and mustache are extremely well done. The pipe is 7″ long.

$85

William Howard Taft is honored in this attractive Bennington-type, 10½″ high bust, which is believed to date from his days in the White House. The brown and black shadings are covered with a high glaze. A fine display piece, and not easily found.

$225

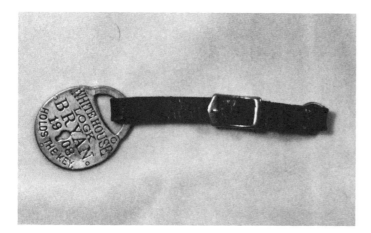

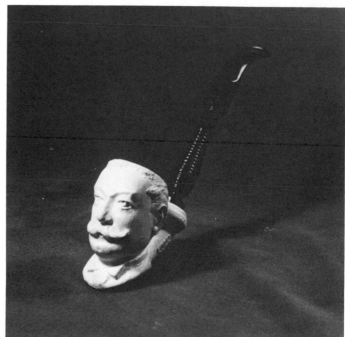

Watch fobs were distributed in abundance during the first decades of this century. This one was a campaign item for William Jennings Bryan in 1908. For the third time, voters decided that they didn't want Bryan to use whatever key he might have had to the White House. The fob is 1¾″ long.

$22

When summer vacation time came, teachers used to give their students little souvenirs to remind them of the importance of a good education and hard work. This one was distributed in Crawford County, Wisconsin, in 1911. The well designed, full-color cover shows all the presidents up through Taft in the border. The back cover pictures the log cabin "Birthplace of Abraham Lincoln." Length, 5¾″.

$18

William Howard Taft is shown here in the form of a toby jug, made in Germany for sale in Washington, D.C., gift shops and elsewhere at the time Taft was in the White House. Taft's rosy cheeks and smile make this a pleasant little memento to place on a shelf in anyone's presidential collection. Height, 5″.

$70

Woodrow Wilson
1913-1921

This match holder, bearing the brownish transfer picture of Woodrow Wilson on both sides, probably was a giveaway at the time Wilson was in office. The flat-back china piece is decorated with two four-leaf clovers and an advertising message that reads, "We appreciate your trade, P.H. Luecke & Co., Giddings, Texas." This item is growing increasingly hard to find. Height, 2″.

$42

President Wilson has a place of honor next to Polish hero Thaddeus Kosciuszko on this full-color framing. Kosciuszko fought with American forces during the Revolutionary War and also was a leader in the fight for Polish independence. The display dates from Wilson's presidency.

$35

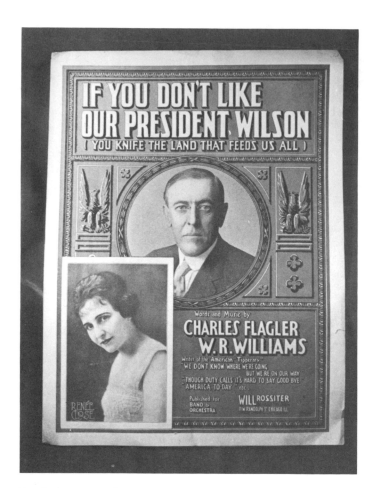

Patriotic support for President Wilson was the overriding theme of this song written during the World War I era. Finding sheet music honoring the presidents has become popular with collectors.

$18

The Panama Canal is featured on this presidential plate which was produced at the time Woodrow Wilson was in office. The geography shows the course of the Canal, and the border pictures all the American presidents through Wilson. The American shield and the flag background add richness to the flow blue type coloring. Diameter, 8¼".

$28

Little china plates adorned with his picture were made while President Woodrow Wilson was in the White House. Today these plates are desirable collectibles. The transfer image of Wilson is the same one that is used on china match holders. The diameter of the plate is 5".

$38

Woodrow Wilson occupied the nation's highest office when this presidential plate was circulated. The White House is shown in color, with all the presidents through Wilson joined in oval portraits around the border. Usually found with much crazing, but a desirable plate, nonetheless. Diameter, 9⅝".

$48

Woodrow Wilson is well portrayed in this attractive blue-and-white tile made by the Mosaic Tile Company of Zanesville, Ohio. Good detail, 3″ high, 3½″ wide.

$40

Support for President Wilson during World War I was the patriotic theme of this tin-framed wall hanging. The length of the frame is 5½″.

$15

This plaster bust of Woodrow Wilson was made by Mooseheart students in Mooseheart, Illinois, as indicated on the bottom. Wilson's name in signature form is shown on the front of the base, and on the back there's the quotation, "The world must be made safe for Democracy." Height, 6″.

$30

This World War I paperweight refers to "The War for Democracy, 1917" and pictures a vigorous-looking President Woodrow Wilson amid eagle and flag decorations in color. Length, 4¼", width, 2¾".

$35

Woodrow Wilson and his vision of world peace caught the imagination of much of the world, even though he did not achieve his goals. Here he is glorified in French on a little metal matchbox holder. Size, 2½" high.

$20

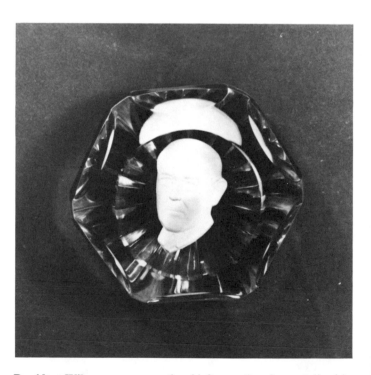

The presidency of Woodrow Wilson is recalled in this little Washington, D.C., souvenir match holder. Wilson and the White House are pictured in color under celluloid on one side, with a bright blue sky over the Capitol on the other. Size, 2¾" x 1½".

$45

President Wilson was among the chief executives immortalized in modern Baccarat paperweights. The quality of this famous old French firm's production is superb, and at least one Baccarat presidential weight belongs in a diversified collection.

$80

Warren G. Harding
1921-1923

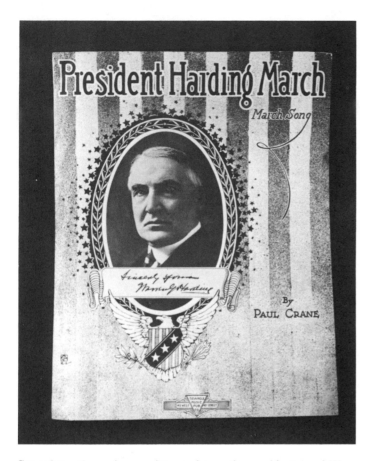

Songs have always been written to honor the presidents, and Warren Harding was no exception. Here's the "President Harding March," which has the usual flattering lyrics, including a line that reads "We have no cause for care, now that you're in the Presidential Chair." At that time, of course, no one could foresee Teapot Dome and Harding's problems with those he had trusted.

$20

James Cox for president and Franklin Roosevelt for vice-president are recalled in this watch fob from the 1920 campaign. Above the oval portraits of the candidates is the wording "E Pluribus Unum" and at the bottom is the campaign slogan, "Our Choice." The fobs are found with both a silver- and gold-plated finish and are not as scarce as another shield-shaped Cox-Roosevelt fob. The one shown here is 1½″ long.

$75

Warren Harding was in the White House when this 3″ "souvenir penny of Kansas City" was made back in the early 1920s. An interesting presidential collectible.

$20

When James Cox ran for president in 1920 on the Democratic ticket with a vice-presidential candidate named Franklin Roosevelt, the number of jugate buttons made was extremely limited—perhaps seventy at most. Last year a one-of-a-kind jugate sold for a record $33,000. The type pictured here also fared well, bringing $3,300. Buttons such as this in first-rate condition will continue to bring even more in the future.

$4,000

Laddie Boy, President Warren Harding's famous pet, is portrayed in this well sculptured metal statue. (The statue also appears in the Color Section.) Held in Laddie Boy's mouth is a copy of the *Marion Star*.

$500

Calvin Coolidge
1923-1929

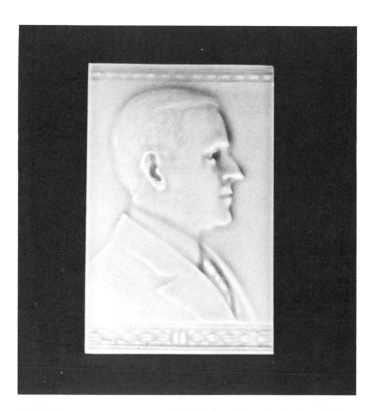

Calvin Coolidge appears on this light blue tile made during the late 1920s when Coolidge served as president. The name "Coolidge" in written form can be faintly discerned on Coolidge's left shoulder. The tile is 2⅞″ wide and 4⅜″ long.

$45

Finding much of anything from the 1924 presidential candidacy of John W. Davis isn't easy, so this little clear glass berry dish made by Hazel-Atlas Glass Company has become an important collectible. The dish, which has fluted sides, was made as a souvenir for a Davis rally in his campaign against Calvin Coolidge. Diameter, 4″.

$55

Grace Coolidge autographed this attractive lithograph of the White House which is neatly framed under glass. A fine remembrance of a gracious first lady. The frame measures 7¼″ x 4¾″.

$45

Calvin Coolidge had a reputation for thrift so what better way to remember him than with a bank? Not too many of these brown-toned pottery banks have survived, and those still around are popular with presidential collectors. The little saying on the front of the base reads, "Do as Coolidge Does—Save." The money slot on the top of Coolidge's head was big enough for a silver dollar. However, to get the money out you had to break the bank—a tragedy in the eyes of today's collectors. Height, 5″.

$95

Herbert Hoover
1929-1933

The 1928 campaign between Al Smith and Herbert Hoover led to the distribution of the souvenir metal busts pictured here. Nothing fancy, but each is fairly well molded, with the candidates' names embossed center front. The busts are 4″ high, 4¾″ wide.

Each **$32**

Shield plaques in rich colors on cardboard were made for the Democratic and Republican candidates in the 1928 presidential election. The GOP team of Herbert Hoover and Charles Curtis are shown at left, with the Happy Warrior, Al Smith, and his running mate, Joseph Robinson, on the right. The plaques are 7½″ high.

Each   **$140**

A **"Hoover for President"** bumper attachment, made for the campaign of 1928. Painted blue and white on tin, 5¼″ wide.

$12

Even matchbook covers make good presidential collectibles. This pair shows Alfred E. Smith featured on the left and the Herbert Hoover and Charles Curtis duo on the right. Many of these campaign boosters were circulated in 1928.

Hoover-Curtis   **$30**
Smith   **$20**

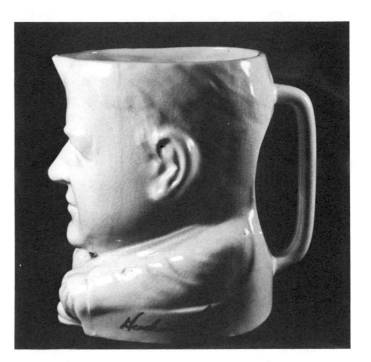

Alfred Smith, the Happy Warrior who lost to Herbert Hoover in the 1928 election, is the subject of this toby pitcher. Made under the Patriotic Products Association Gold Medal China label, the 7″ pitcher is a companion to the Hoover toby. A popular campaign item, but found less often than the Hoover pitcher.

$65

The 1928 campaign between Herbert Hoover and Al Smith is brought to mind by this Hoover toby pitcher. The bottom has the shield label of the Patriotic Products Association and the words, "Gold Metal China, O.C. Co., Made in U.S, Patent Applied For." As in the case of the Smith toby pitcher, the facial likeness is skillfully done. Collectors who are lucky still find these tobies occasionally at flea markets and, more often, in shops. Height, 7″.

$60

When the ladies powdered their noses they were reminded of the importance of their vote by this compact made for candidate Al Smith in the 1928 presidential election. The diameter is 2½″.

$75

Hoover is pictured here on a wooden paperweight that was made around the time of his presidency. The angular-shaped weight is 3″ high.

$28

107

The center medallion of this token-like, stacked paperweight pictures George Washington and President Herbert Hoover in bas-relief. Previous presidents and the years they took office are shown on the other "tokens." Width, 5¼".

$38

A souvenir medal of Herbert Hoover's inauguration on March 4, 1929. The new president didn't know it then, but before the year was over the nation would be rocked by financial disaster on Wall Street. Length, 2¼".

$32

A second term for Herbert Hoover was advocated in this old oilcloth tire cover made for the 1932 election. However, with the Depression deepening, voters had lost confidence in Hoover and turned to his Democratic opponent, Franklin D. Roosevelt. The tire cover is an unusual and interesting memento of the campaign.

$150

Franklin D. Roosevelt
1933·1945

This Franklin Roosevelt pottery pitcher made by the Stangl Pottery firm of Trenton, New Jersey, is believed to date from Roosevelt's first campaign for the presidency. The smiling face is shown in bas-relief on one side, with the familiar "Happy Days Are Here Again" impressed within a rectangle on the reverse side. Speckled brown coloring emphasizes Roosevelt's face. The Stangl name is impressed on the base of this amusing 7¼"-high pitcher, which is part of a set with matching mugs.

$90

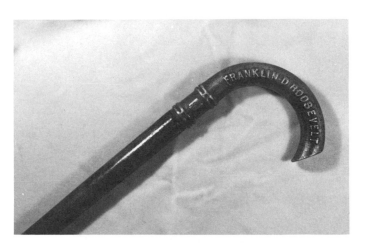

Canes were fine for promoting most presidential candidates, but for the handicapped Franklin D. Roosevelt, they certainly weren't appropriate. Yet this one was made for FDR's 1932 campaign. The other side of the handle says "For President," and shows the "32" date. The metal cane attachment is about 8" long.

$75

"The New Deal" slogan and the embossed image of Franklin Roosevelt in a shield on the side of this tan-colored, barrel-shaped mug offer a variation of the happy days theme. Made early in Roosevelt's presidency. Many collectors like to get a half dozen or more of these and serve beer to their guests. Height, 4".

$15

Getting the nation back to work was the general theme stressed on this 1933 lampshade honoring the social programs of President Roosevelt. The shade shows a determined-looking Roosevelt, with decorations including the NRA symbol, a farmer at work in the fields, a train and ship, and smoke coming out of busy factories. A hard-to-find item. The shade is 5" high.

$55

"**Happy Days** Are Here Again" is the theme of this beer-barrel-shaped green pottery mug with a heavy glaze. Made for the end of Prohibition when Franklin Roosevelt was in the White House. The slogans on such mugs always will be associated with memories of FDR. Height, 4¾".

$22

Prohibition ended, "Happy Days" mugs were circulated early in the presidency of Franklin Roosevelt. This one is white, picturing a beer keg on one side and the words "Happy Days Are Here Again" on the other. The bottom is marked "General Beverage Sales Co." Height, 5".

$20

After Franklin Roosevelt took control of the nation's destiny in the 1932 election, little metal statues of FDR began appearing in the stores. This one shows a young Roosevelt and carries the message, "Our New Deal President, Franklin D. Roosevelt, 1933."

$10

One of the most commonly found reminders of the days of Franklin Roosevelt is this little "Happy Days" shot glass decorated with the Democratic donkey.

$8

Made of tin, this little "Happy Days" bank has found its way into many presidential collections. Another reminder that Prohibition was repealed when Franklin Roosevelt came into office. Height, 4″.

$8

These little metal statues were popular during the Chicago World's Fair. Marked on the front "Franklin D. Roosevelt, 1933." Height, 4½″.

$15

Young and handsome, Franklin Roosevelt is pictured in full color on these wall plaques, probably made around the time that he took office. The large celluloid has a diameter of 9″, while the other is 4⅝″ x 3⅝″. A black label shows that the large plaque was made by the P.N. Company of Chicago.

Large $45
Small $18

A companion piece for the large Franklin Roosevelt "Happy Days Are Here Again" pitcher is this barrel-shaped Stangl Pottery mug, embossed with FDR's confident likeness. Signed "Stangl" on the bottom. Height, 4".

$38

Smoking his familiar cigar and smiling, Al Smith was one of the Democratic superstars at the time of the 1932 presidential election. The signed Stangl pottery mug shown here was part of a set that went with the large Stangl Roosevelt "Happy Days" pitcher. Height, 4".

$38

Inexpensive metal lamps and clocks showing FDR at the helm as "The Man of the Hour" still are offered for sale frequently in shops and at flea markets. They were made during his first term. The lamp shown, with an apricot-colored globe, stands 16" high.

$35

Alfred Landon, who went down to a crushing defeat when he ran against President Franklin Roosevelt in 1936, was publicized as the candidate to elect in this brightly decorated, red, white, and blue coffee mug. The decorations include a flag-type motif and the wording "Alf Landon for President." A scarce and attractive item, 4" high.

$45

A magnificent marquetry table, featuring George Washington, the American eagle, crossed flags, and a shield, was made for the 1876 Centennial. Fine workmanship and typical Victorian decorations characterize this unusual piece of Centennial furniture honoring the nation's first president. The table stands 31″ high. The top has a diameter of 24½″.

$3,000

William Howard Taft and his vice-presidential candidate, James Schoolcraft Sherman, are pictured on this beautiful full-color "Grand Old Party Standard Bearers" tin plate made in 1908 by the Meek Company of Coshocton, Ohio. Enhanced by gorgeous color and handsome design, the plate shows all Republicans who carried the GOP banner from 1856 to 1908 and is decorated with shields, the American flag, and the White House. It still appears on the market frequently, and because of its quality and historic excellence ranks as a bargain. Diameter, 9½″.

$85

William McKinley is shown in bas-relief on this unusual German beer stein. The president's image is lifelike, with realistic features and coloring. The German moldmaker misspelled McKinley's name however, making it "MacKinley." The error only adds more interest to this desirable presidential item. It is 5¾" high.

$100

When it comes to political campaign umbrellas it's hard to beat the dramatic flair shown in those that were made in 1900, when William McKinley sought reelection with his running mate, Theodore Roosevelt. When these are found in good condition, buyers are always available.

$200

William McKinley and his running mate, Garret Hobart, are pictured on the sides of this large water pitcher that was made for the 1896 campaign against William Jennings Bryan. The facsimile signatures of McKinley and Hobart appear beneath their transfer images. Hard to find and an excellent addition to any presidential collection, the pitcher is 10" tall.

$300

Small toby jugs made in the likeness of Franklin Delano Roosevelt are sought after by presidential collectors. Some are white, others are tan. These attractive ceramic souvenirs are 3¾″ high.

$30

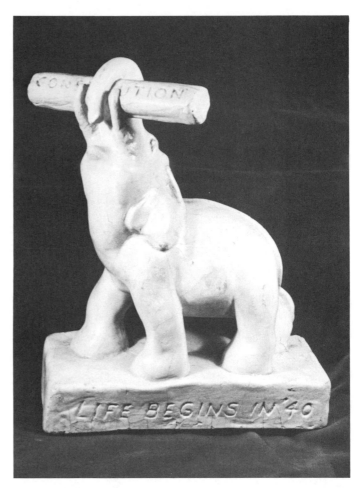

"Life Begins in '40" was the slogan used frequently in 1940 when Wendell Willkie unsuccessfully tried to head off a third term for President Franklin Roosevelt. This plaster elephant carried the slogan on the base, with the word "Constitution" inscribed on the log the GOP elephant is holding with its trunk. The campaign elephants were made in 1939 in Green Bay, Wisconsin.

$30

Those who wondered whether Franklin Roosevelt intended to break precedent and seek a third term received their answer in this amusing little hard-rubber FDR head nodder. The back of the campaign item asks the question, "Going to run for a third term?" For an answer, you set the rocker-like head on a table, then tap the chin. This sets the head to nodding about a dozen times in a definite "yes" manner. An interesting presidential memento.

$48

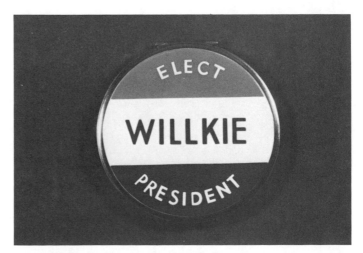

Wendell Willkie's bid to win the presidency in the 1940 campaign prompted the production of many promotional items, including this red, white, and blue compact with the slogan, "Elect Willkie President." The inside is marked "Volupte, U.S.A." Diameter, 3″.

$30

Wendell Willkie's acceptance speech on August 17, 1940, in Elwood, Indiana, is recalled in this red, white, and blue star-decorated tumbler, which also pictures the candidate. Height, 4½".

$12

Words showing that he was ready for anything are featured on this little milk glass campaign ashtray for 1940 GOP presidential candidate, Wendell Willkie. The diameter is 3½".

$10

Flags of the Allied nations are shown in color as a border decoration for this attractive plate honoring President Franklin Roosevelt. Although not marked on the back, the plate appears to have been made by the Salem China Company. Diameter, 10⅞".

$38

A handsome gold-decorated border adds to the dignity of this fine souvenir plate picturing President Franklin Roosevelt. Large, with a diameter of nearly 11", the plate was made by the Salem China Company. The transfer image of Roosevelt is reddish brown.

$35

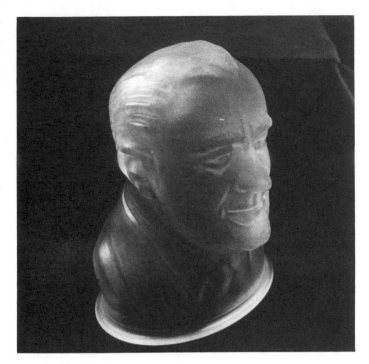

Large enough to be lighted from within, frosted glass bust of Franklin Roosevelt is a somewhat eerie portrayal of our thirty-second president. The bust stands 9″ tall and has a 5″ base. The facial features are not as fine as they might be, and the skin is not smooth. But in some respects, these differences only add interest.

$100

Franklin D. Roosevelt made many stirring speeches during his years in office, and this Wedgwood blue-and-white mug commemorates his words, "This can be done, it must be done, it will be done." The Wedgwood image of FDR, however, shows him to be somewhat heavier than most Americans remember. On the reverse side of the 4¼″-high mug is the embossed symbol of an eagle.

$75

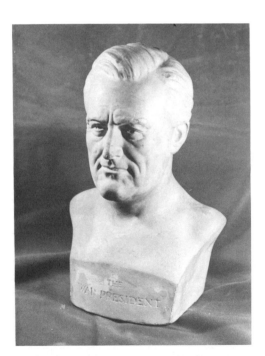

Franklin D. Roosevelt is the subject of this clear glass bust candy container with a frosted finish. The features are reasonably accurate, and the hollow base helps create interesting facial shadows when the bust is placed in the light. It stands 5″ high, and has "F.D. Roosevelt" embossed on the base.

$65

President Franklin Roosevelt looks young and strong on this heavy plaster bust entitled "The War President." The reverse side is marked. "To Hon. Frances Perkins, Miniature replica of bust of President Roosevelt, Presented to the People of the United States by the AHEPA." Frances Perkins served FDR for four terms as Secretary of Labor. The unusual statue is 10″ high.

$25

123

Two ashtrays made with the likeness of President Franklin Roosevelt. The one on the left is a souvenir of Warm Springs, Georgia, site of "The Little White House," and the other was made in England. The round ashtray has a diameter of 5″; the square one is 4″ x 4″.

Round   **$8**
Square   **$10**

A **memorial** tile of Franklin Roosevelt, 6″ x 6″, has a chronolgy of the important dates of his life on the reverse side. The dates are bordered in black and bear the name of the Kemper-Thomas Company, Cincinnati, Ohio.

$15

An **Indiana** state Democratic convention medal for delegates in 1946 honored the memory of Franklin Roosevelt with the message, "Carry On." The same slogan had been used in Roosevelt's reelection campaign. The medal is 3¼″ long.

$10

This **deep** green bottle with an almost carnival glass-type finish pictures a jaunty Franklin Roosevelt with a hat and a long cigarette holder jutting from his mouth. His name and the dates of his birth and death are on the front. On the reverse side is a quote from a famous speech, his term in office, and his signature. A commemorative made by the Wheaton Glass Company, Millville, New Jersey. Height. 7¾″.

$16

Looking youthful and strong, Franklin Roosevelt was honored on this fine presidential plate designed for wall display. The plate, which has a green wreath border and probably was made after his death, was manufactured in Holland. Diameter, 10⅜″.

$40

Harry Truman
1945-1953

That famous Truman look is well captured on this souvenir-shop china plate from Washington, D.C. Truman plates usually attract the attention of collectors more readily than many of the others because mementos from his presidency are harder to find. Diameter, 7⅛″.

$15

President Harry Truman is remembered in this pale blue Wedgwood jasperware sweet dish made in England for the American market. The gutsy determination that people think of when they recall Truman is captured in the excellent facial detail. Diameter, 4⅜".

$12

They were waving pennants for a confident Thomas E. Dewey in 1948, but American voters responded instead to the "give 'em hell" campaign conducted by Harry Truman. Today the pennants are reminders of that colorful campaign.

$22

The Capitol looms in the background on this tie made for Thomas Dewey's 1948 campaign against Harry Truman.

$15

Dwight Eisenhower
1953-1961

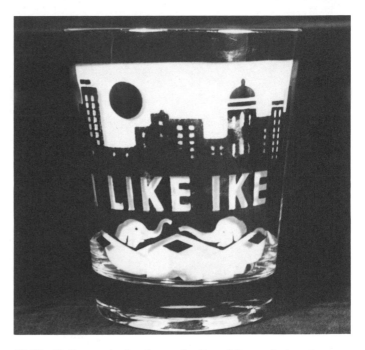

"I like Ike" was the battle cry for Republicans during the campaigns of Dwight D. Eisenhower. This tumbler carries the slogan and a decoration that emphasizes that Ike would best serve the interests of rural as well as urban voters. Height, 4¾".

$22

Neckties made for the 1952 presidential campaign pictured two Republicans seeking the nomination, war hero Gen. Dwight Eisenhower and United States Senator Robert Taft. Eisenhower was nominated on the first ballot and went on to serve two terms in the White House.

Each   **$15**

Smokers were not ignored in the campaign to get Dwight Eisenhower elected president. This brightly packaged and still unopened pack of cigarettes pictures a smiling Ike along with his well-remembered slogan. The campaign packs were produced by the Tobacco Blending Corporation of Louisville, Kentucky.

$12

Eisenhower's winning smile has made this campaign bandanna popular with collectors. The coloring is red, white, and blue. These are still found at bargain prices.

$22

A starred border decorates this attractive likeness of President Dwight Eisenhower commemorating his inauguration January 20, 1953. The reverse marking shows the plate was decorated by Delano Studios of New York. Diameter, 10⅝".

$16

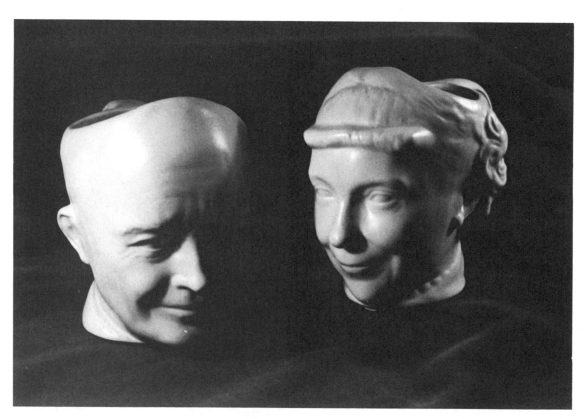

Ike and Mamie toby mugs used to be found often at flea markets but in recent years have all but disappeared. They make an excellent addition to any presidential collection since they exude a "first family" image much more dramatically than the more common souvenir plates. The President Eisenhower toby is 5" high, while Mamie is 4½".

Each **$22**

A **metal bank** made in the image of President Eisenhower still turns up with frequency in antique shops and at flea markets. The bank is 5″ high.

$12

For those Americans who like to say "I'll drink to that," there was a whiskey bottle made to commemorate the inauguration of Dwight Eisenhower in 1953. The front of the bottle pictures the Capitol and the back lists the names of the presidents, their birthdates, home states, and year of inauguration. A worthwhile memento, 11¼″ high.

$18

The little schoolhouse in Ripon, Wisconsin, where the Republican party is said to have been born in 1854 is honored by this plate produced in 1954 when Dwight Eisenhower was president. Abraham Lincoln was the first elected Republican president, so he is pictured on the party Centennial plate with Eisenhower. Information about the schoolhouse is given on the reverse side. The plate, with a diameter of 9¼″, was made by the Homer Laughlin firm.

$10

Americans liked Ike and they liked Mamie, and that's why the plate picturing them under the heading "America's First Family" was popular with buyers when the Eisenhowers were in the White House. The transfer is in full color, and the plate, which has a 9″-diameter, has a gold trim on the border.

$15

All the presidents through Dwight Eisenhower are pictured on this china plate sold in souvenir shops during Eisenhower's two terms. Diameter, 7¼″.

$10

John F. Kennedy
1961-1963

President John F. Kennedy and Mrs. Kennedy are pictured on this little souvenir china creamer marketed in Washington, D.C., gift shops. It stands 3¾″ high.

$8

John F. Kennedy's smiling face is used on this clear glass tumbler to express the political sentiments of the "Van Buren County Democrats." Height, 4½″.

$12

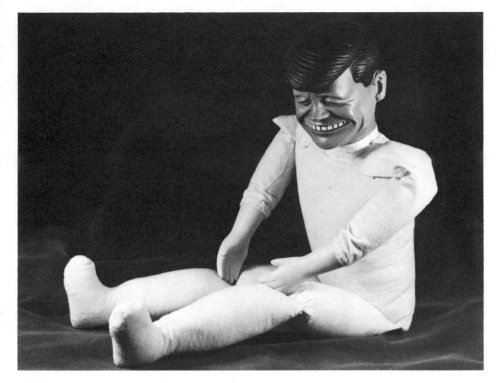

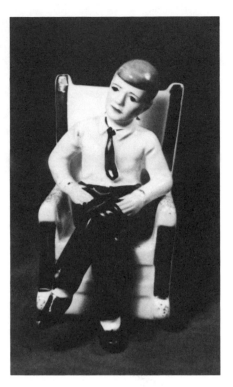

A smiling John F. Kennedy doll which stands more than 20″ tall is a favorite with many collectors who specialize in JFK items. The doll has a composition head; the body, except for the hands, is cloth. The Kennedy doll looks great in a tuxedo.

$50

An amusing presidential collectible is this Japanese-made salt and pepper set designed to represent John F. Kennedy sitting in his famous rocker. The holes for pouring the salt are in Kennedy's back, while the pepper holes are on the back on the rocker. An interesting souvenir.

$25

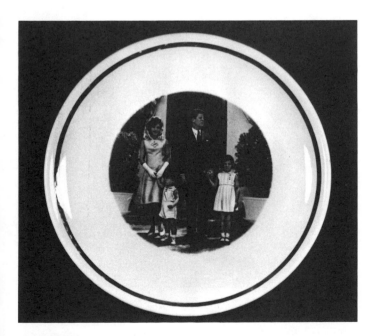

Many Americans recall the Camelot days of the John F. Kennedy presidency in a family scene such as this one. The president and his wife, Jackie, are shown in color with Caroline and little John-John. Diameter, 9″.

$18

Another of the many souvenir china dishes that were made when President John F. Kennedy and his wife, Jackie, brought youth and beauty to the White House. This heart-shaped dish, with the Kennedys pictured in color, was made in Japan. The width is 5″.

$8

John F. Kennedy and Jackie salt and pepper shakers sell well to presidential collectors. Here are two types. The more common round shakers are shown at the top; the flat-sided monument-type are pictured on the bottom. The round shakers are 2¾″ high, while the others are 2″ tall.

Round, pair **$4**
Flat, pair **$8**

Those who collect the presidential plates will like this one featuring John F. Kennedy. Although the likenesses of some of the presidents may be faulted, the color is good and the plate is attractive. Diameter, 10⅛″.

$16

Personality bottle tops were made in the shape of United States presidents. This one showing John F. Kennedy is still in the original box. Made in Japan and 5″ high.

$9

Sets of tumblers were sold as a memorial to the assassinated John F. Kennedy. This one pictured Kennedy in blue, framed by a wreath, with the dates 1917-1963. The back is decorated with PT-Boat 109, Kennedy's rocking chair, his "Ask Not What Your Country Can Do for You . . ." quote, and the eternal flame. A thoughtful piece, and appropriate for any presidential collection. Height, 5½″.

$12

Tin serving trays that recall the Kennedy years in the White House were made as a memorial to the assassinated president. The trays, with an 8¼″ diameter, feature the full-color pictures of John F. Kennedy and his wife, Jacqueline, on cardboard.

Pair   **$22**

A memorial tumbler shows the enameled bust of John F. Kennedy, the dates of his birth and death, and quotes from his famous 1961 inaugural address.

$15

Inexpensive mourning plates were turned out in abundance after the assassination of President John F. Kennedy. The one shown at the top has a diameter of 7″. The diameter of the other is 8″.

Each   **$7**

The assassinated Kennedy brothers, John and Robert, are shown on this color plate that is a worthy additon to any presidential collection. John Kennedy was slain while in the White House. Robert was gunned down while campaigning for the presidency. Their deaths are a tragic reminder of the violence that too frequently befalls the nation's leaders. Diameter, 7".

$15

John F. Kennedy is portrayed in this modern, metal-ringed glass paperweight, one of a series. Good likeness of Kennedy in bas-relief. Diameter, 3".

$22

Lyndon Johnson
1963-1969

The initials "LBJ" and the cowboy hat tell the presidential collector that this is a bumper sticker made for Lyndon Baines Johnson, our thirty-sixth president. The size is 7¼" long, 3⅝" wide. Colors are yellow and black.

$2

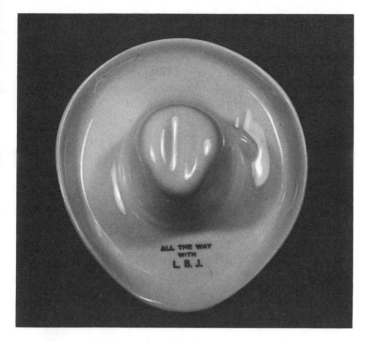

An ashtray in the shape of LBJ's hat makes an interesting and relatively inexpensive souvenir. The hat is 6″ long and 5″ wide.

$12

When Nelson Rockefeller made a strong presidential bid in 1964 this umbrella was one of his campaign items. The umbrella is brightly colored, and Rockefeller's picture is shown in the panels. It bears the slogan, "Rockefeller for President." Height, 30″.

$48

With "Super LBJ" on the cover, here's a comic book giving an imaginative portrayal of the presidency. As it says on the back cover, it's a case of "guns, butter and laughs." An amusing addition for any presidential collector. Dimensions, 10″ x 7″.

$12

Lyndon B. Johnson is the subject of this presidential bottle top still in the original box. We're not sure whether the Japanese designer really captured the LBJ look, but it's now a collectible. Height, 5″.

$9

Presidents up to and including Lyndon Johnson are pictured on items that were made as souvenirs during the years that LBJ was in the White House. This teapot, which shows the presidential images in color, is 5¼″ high. It was imported in 1966 by the Chadwick-Miller firm, as the backstamp indicates.

$12

President Johnson was pictured on many souvenirs sold in Washington, D.C., shops during his years in the White House. This little full-color pitcher is an example of the type of item available at the time, 3¾″ high.

$10

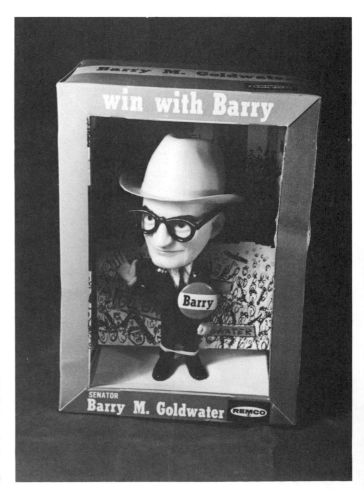

An LBJ belt buckle dramatized the lifestyle of President Lyndon Johnson, who enjoyed entertaining friends at the LBJ Ranch in Texas. Size, 2″ x 3¼″.

$8

The "Win with Barry" slogan on the box of this 1964 dashboard doll of Senator Barry Goldwater didn't get him elected, but it helped preserve his image. A similar dashboard doll was made for Lyndon Johnson. The boxes of these dolls also were attractively decorated by Remco Industries, Incorporated, Harrison, New Jersey. The boxed doll is 7¼″ high, 5¼″ wide.

$12

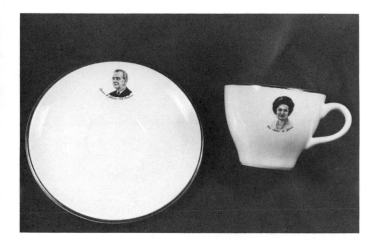

Both LBJ and Lady Bird are pictured on this cup and saucer combination made as a souvenir while Lyndon Johnson was in the White House. The cup is 2¾" high, and the plate has a diameter of 6".

$10

President Lyndon Johnson and his wife, Lady Bird, are captured in a rather formal pose on this souvenir china plate. The transfer print is in the customary color on this plate, which has a diameter of 9".

$15

A tin serving tray with a cardboard color picture of President Johnson is among the collectibles that still can be easily found. The same kind of plate-size tray was made for John F. Kennedy.

$10

A presidential plate showing the former chief executives in brown transfer prints was made with Lyndon Johnson in the center. Green leaves decorate the center circle and border. An interesting plate, larger than most, with a diameter of 10¼".

$16

Richard Nixon
1969-1974

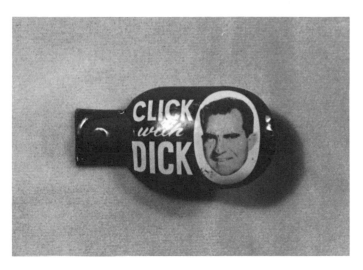

Voters were urged to "Click with Dick" in this little Richard Nixon campaign giveaway. Other shapes of clickers also were used. Blue and white, 2½" long.

$8

Autographed by Richard Nixon and his wife, Pat, this 1968 Lincoln Day dinner ticket is framed against a newspaper artist's sketch of a school gymnasium that provided a typical setting for many campaign speeches that year. In November of 1968, Nixon was elected president.

$100

This 1968 campaign bank championed the cause of Richard Nixon and Spiro Agnew. On one side is embossed "Nixon 68 Agnew." The other is marked "GOP." A good little remembrance of that election, especially when coupled with the companion Democratic donkey bank. Iron, and just 2¾" high.

$35

When Hubert Humphrey and Edmund Muskie teamed up to oppose Richard Nixon and Spiro Agnew in the 1968 presidential contest, these little iron donkey banks appeared as campaign items. They have been moving steadily into the hands of collectors, but some still can be found. One side reads, "Humphrey Muskie 68" and the other carries the word, "Democrat." Height, 4¼".

$30

The only presidential tandem in history individually driven from office was boosted on this campaign jewelry made for Richard Nixon and Spiro Agnew. That alone should make it collectible. The pin is 1¾" high.

$8

Both the figural bottles and the red, white, and blue boxes are eye-catching and well done in the case of the Wheaton Company Nuline campaign items produced in 1968. This photo shows the GOP elephant, with Richard Nixon embossed on one side and Spiro Agnew, the vice-presidential nominee, on the other. The base is marked "Republican Campaign." The color is amber, and the bottle stands 7" high.

$15

A corked jug was made as an inauguration souvenir for Richard Nixon and Spiro Agnew. The 4¾" jugs carry the Nixon and Agnew names and a picture of the Capitol dome.

$18

Hubert H. Humphrey and Edmund Muskie are embossed on the sides of this rich green glass figural campaign bottle made in 1968 by the Wheaton Company in Millville, New Jersey. The medallion images of the candidates also bear the 1968 date. Good items, and still often underpriced on today's market. Height, 7".

$15

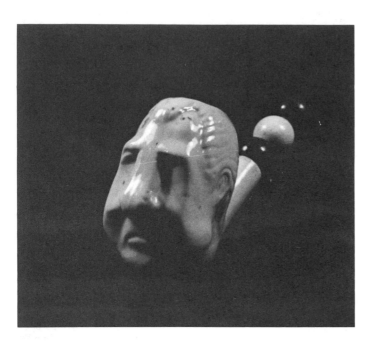

Spiro Agnew's troubled days as vice-president are recalled by this toy pipe made for blowing soap bubbles. The bowl is ceramic and the colored balls on the stem are made of wood. A good item for those who appreciate the historic significance of the disintegration of the presidency of Richard Nixon. From end to end, the little pipe measures 4¼".

$35

Spiro Agnew watches definitely have become collectible, especially after the shameful manner in which he and President Nixon both were forced to leave office. The watch is about 1½" long.

$45

Pre-Watergate days in the White House were satisfying ones for President Richard Nixon and his wife, Pat. Their smiling image is shown in color on a typical souvenir china plate with a diameter of 9".

$15

The Bobby Kennedy presidential boom was brief, but it lasted long enough for these red, white, and blue mugs to be made for his 1968 campaign. He was assassinated in California just when his effort to win the presidency seemed to be gaining momentum. The mug is 4" high.

$9

This Nixon toothpick holder was made as a Bicentennial piece—but President Nixon had been driven from office as a result of the Watergate scandal before the national celebration ever began. It's an attractive presidential souvenir nevertheless, showing the bas-relief image of Nixon with George Washington and an American Indian pictured elsewhere around the sides. Stars also appear at the top edge and near the pedestal base. The bottom of this amethyst piece, which is 2½″ high, is marked "Original Bob St. Clair, 1776-1976."

$20

Richard Nixon is centered in a plate that was made for the souvenir shops during his troubled presidency. Portraits of all the presidents are in color, and the 9″ plate has a gold border edging.

$15

All the shenanigans associated with the Watergate scandal are recalled in this amusing card game appropriately named, "The Watergate Scandal." Some day collectors will explain to their grandchildren what Watergate was all about—and the cards will provide helpful graphics.

$6

141

Gerald Ford
1974-1977

His time in office was short, so collectibles from the presidency of Gerald Ford are not around in abundance. This little gift shop mug identifies him as the thirty-eighth president and lists his August 9, 1974, inauguration date. Height, 3¾″.

$22

A smiling President Gerald Ford and Mrs. Ford are portrayed in a color transfer in the center of this Washington, D.C., souvenir plate. The plate, with a 9¼″ diameter, has gold edging. Items from the Ford presidency will be hard to find in the future.

$15

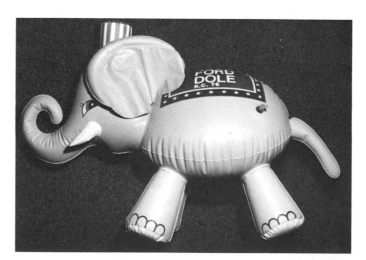

Souvenir platemakers also produced a presidential plate for Gerald Ford. Shown in the center, he is surrounded in the usual manner by all his predecessors. The historic value of these modestly priced plates is enhanced because most of them carry not only portraits of the presidents but the years that they served. Diameter, 10″.

$18

An air-filled, plastic GOP elephant sang the praises of the Ford-Dole team in 1976. This campaign collectible is about 14″ high.

$12

Jimmy Carter
1977-1981

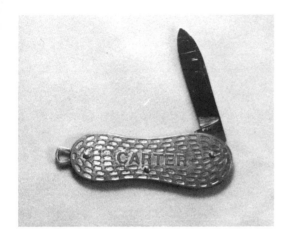

The peanut in all forms was glorified during the Bicentennial year campaign of Jimmy Carter. Here's a little peanut-shaped, one-bladed jackknife made by Taylor Cutlery, Kingsport, Tennessee. One side of the peanut has the name "Carter" and the other says, "Mr. Peanut, Nov. 2, 1976." A good campaign memento, 3″ long (with the blade closed).

$22

The handles of two canes made for Jimmy Carter's successful bid for the presidency in 1976 reflect the respectable quality of these recent campaign collectibles. One stresses the background of the candidate as a Georgia peanut farmer, and the other is similar to a cane made for the 1932 campaign of Franklin Roosevelt.

Each $30

A grinning peanut mug was made as a souvenir of Jimmy Carter's years as the country's leader. The peanut handle, the Carter smile, and the boots are all reminders of his presidency. Height, 5¼″.

$5

The adaptability of the presidential plate manufacturers is shown in this plate which was made in Japan. At the center top is Gerald Ford—with his White House departure date still not listed. To make the plate current after the election, Carter's picture was pasted on above the American eagle.

$10

Coffee mugs picturing the presidents have been popular in recent years. This one shows Jimmy Carter with the transfer in color and identifies Carter as our thirty-ninth president. Height, 3⅝″.

$12

The shadowed features of President Jimmy Carter are portrayed on this souvenir plate. The president is pictured in color. Diameter, 10¼″.

$10

A peanut holder (or planter) was made after Jimmy Carter had been elected to the presidency. The name "Mel Tiess" is stamped on the back of this humorous collectible. Marketed in plaster shops, the peanut holders also have moved onto the tables at flea markets and shops emphasizing collectibles. Height, 8¾″.

Painted **$22**

Smiling President Jimmy Carter, wearing his tan cardigan sweater, is portrayed here as a 16½″ plaster statue, apparently offering a peanut to the nation. Fine coloring and good flesh tones on the face make this an interesting collectible. It was made by Esco Products in 1977 and is sure to rise in value.

$45

One of the hits at the 1980 Democratic convention was this cleverly made "Teddy" Kennedy bear. Those who supported the presidential bid of Senator Edward Kennedy had great fun with these bears, almost as much fun in fact as do the political collectors. A tag on the side of the "Teddy" bear, manufactured in Los Angeles, reads, "Teddy Bear, 1980, A Unique Collectible, Wes Soderstrom, Woodland HIlls, Calif., P.O. Box 60 91365." About 17″ high.

$50

The Carter-Mondale campaign team is pictured on this pocket watch shown with a Carter watch fob. The watches, particularly, should increase in value in the years ahead.

Watch **$22**
Fob **$6**

Ronald Reagan
1981

Made for the Republican National Convention in Kansas City in 1976, this Ronald Reagan glass has joined the list of collectibles. Reagan's image and the printing are frosted on clear glass. It is 3¼″ high.

$8

145

President Ronald Reagan and Vice-President George Bush are pictured on this star-trimmed, gold-edged, flag-waving plate made to observe Reagan's inauguration. An attractive souvenir bearing the inaugural seal, the 10¼″ plate was made in a limited edition on fine porcelain china by Wildlife Art, Ltd. of California. The art is from a painting by Douglas VanHowd.

$50

Two postcards, one showing President Reagan and Mrs. Reagan in a parody of a long-familiar painting, and the other picturing President Reagan and his vice-president, George Bush, have been widely circulated. Also shown is a Reagan-Bush jackknife. These items, along with a wide assortment of buttons, are among the current collectibles.

Reagan-Mrs. Reagan	$1
Reagan-Bush	$1
Knife	$5

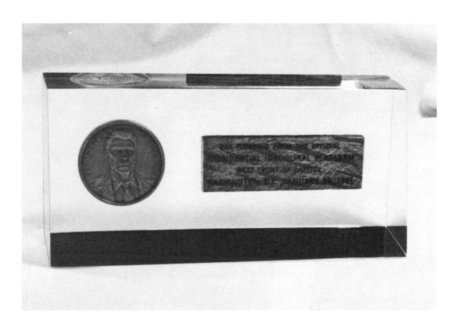

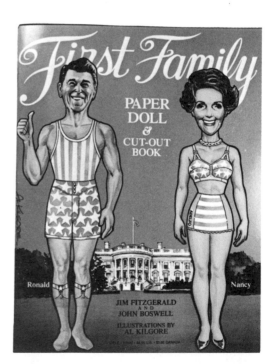

How about a paperweight that captures forever an actual piece of the oak platform on which Ronald Reagan and other dignitaries stood when he was inaugurated on January 20, 1981? Hall-Schuman & Associates of Verona, Pennsylvania, offered such an authenticated souvenir, with a 3″ x 1″ piece of the flooring, plus a copper inaugural medal encased in Lucite. It seems likely that these will increase in value over the years. The original price was just $28 plus shipping. Attractive, 6¼″ long and 3″ high.

$30

The "First Family" paper doll and cutout book showing President and Mrs. Reagan on the cover has been popular with collectors everywhere. It is 9″ x 12″ and provides some delightful outfits plus decorations for the Oval Office. Published by Dell Publishing Company, 1 Dag Hammarskjold Plaza, New York, New York.

$4.95

A Frankoma elephant carries a 1981 date and the names of Reagan and Bush. The other side of the elephant has the familiar "GOP." Height, 4″

$8

Jellybeans gained national prominence when President Ronald Reagan took office. One of the more interesting collectibles with that tasty theme is a ceramic "Jellybean White House." The top lifts off and inside, of course, are jellybeans. A label on the base of the 5½″ x 4⅝″ souvenir shows that it was distributed by Ego Enterprises of Barrington, Illinois. Because the knob is a little slippery to grasp, the all-important tops may suffer breakage over the years. Those that survive intact will become more desirable when the Reagan years fade into history.

$18

Collecting buttons can be great fun, and there are thousands who do it. This modest assortment includes many buttons worth only $.75 to $1. A few would sell for $15 or more. The highest-priced button is second from the top at left, picturing Bryan and Stevenson in 1900 and is worth around $40. The display also shows some buttons that have no genuine campaign roots, but were made to be sold to persons who enjoy them and do not always insist upon authenticity. However, "fakes" or reproductions definitely are not wanted by most serious collectors.

The Presidents and Many of the Also-rans

Over the years numerous obscure candidates have sought the office of the presidency. This list makes no claim to include them all, but shows the names of many who were familiar to a wide audience of the nation's voters.

1789

George Washington, president
John Adams, vice-president

Others receiving votes: John Jay, Robert Harrison, John Rutledge, John Hancock, George Clinton, Samuel Huntington, John Milton, James Armstrong, Benjamin Lincoln, Edward Telfair

1792

George Washington, president
John Adams, vice-president

Others receiving votes: George Clinton, Thomas Jefferson, Aaron Burr

1796

John Adams, president
Thomas Jefferson, vice-president

Others receiving votes: Thomas Pinckney, Aaron Burr, Samuel Adams, Oliver Ellsworth, George Clinton, John Jay, James Iredell, John Henry, Samuel Johnson, George Washington, Charles Pinckney

1800

Thomas Jefferson, president
Aaron Burr, vice-president

Others receiving votes: John Adams, Charles Pinckney, John Jay

1804

Thomas Jefferson, president
George Clinton, vice-president

Others receiving votes: Charles Pinckney

1808

James Madison, president
George Clinton, vice-president

Others receiving votes: Charles Pinckney

1812

James Madison, president
Elbridge Gerry, vice-president

Others receiving votes: Dewitt Clinton

1816

James Monroe, president
Daniel Tompkins, vice-president

Others receiving votes: Rufus King

1820

James Monroe, president
Daniel Tompkins, vice-president

Others receiving votes: John Quincy Adams

1824

John Quincy Adams, president
John Calhoun, vice-president

Others receiving votes: Andrew Jackson, William H. Crawford, Henry Clay

1828

Andrew Jackson, president
John C. Calhoun, vice-president

Others receiving votes: John Quincy Adams

1832

Andrew Jackson, president
Martin Van Buren, vice-president

Others receiving votes: Henry Clay, John Floyd, William Wirt

1836

Martin Van Buren, president
Richard M. Johnson, vice-president

> Others receiving votes: William H. Harrison, Daniel Webster, Hugh L. White, William P. Mangum

1840

William H. Harrison, president
John Tyler, vice-president

> Others receiving votes: Martin Van Buren, James G. Birney

1844

James K. Polk, president
George M. Dallas, vice-president

> Others receiving votes: Henry Clay, James G. Birney

1848

Zachary Taylor, president
Millard Fillmore, vice-president

> Others receiving votes: Lewis Cass, Martin Van Buren

1852

Franklin Pierce, president
William R. King, vice-president

> Others receiving votes: Winfield Scott, John P. Hale

1856

James Buchanan, president
John C. Breckinridge, vice-president

> Others receiving votes: John C. Fremont, Millard Fillmore

1860

Abraham Lincoln, president
Hannibal Hamlin, vice-president

> Others receiving votes: John C. Breckinridge, Stephen Douglas, John Bell, Jefferson Davis

1864

Abraham Lincoln, president
Andrew Johnson, vice-president

> Others receiving votes: George B. McClellan

1868

Ulysses S. Grant, president
Schuyler Colfax, vice-president

> Others receiving votes: Horatio Seymour

1872

Ulysses S. Grant, president
Henry Wilson, vice-president

> Others receiving votes: Horace Greeley, Charles O'Conor, James Black, Thomas Hendricks, B. Gratz Brown, Charles J. Jenkins, David Davis, Victoria Woodhull

1876

Rutherford B. Hayes, president
William A. Wheeler, vice-president

> Others receiving votes: Samuel J. Tilden, Peter Cooper, Green C. Smith, James B. Walker

1880

James A. Garfield, president
Chester A. Arthur, vice-president

> Others receiving votes: Winfield S. Hancock, James B. Weaver, Neal Dow, John W. Phelps

1884

Grover Cleveland, president
Thomas A. Hendricks, vice-president

> Others receiving votes: James G. Blaine, John P. St. John, Benjamin F. Butler, P. D. Wiggington, Mrs. Belva Lockwood, Samuel C. Pomeroy

1888

Benjamin Harrison, president
Levi P. Morton, vice-president

> Others receiving votes: Grover Cleveland, Clinton B. Fisk, Alson J. Streeter, R.H. Cowdry, James L. Curtis, Mrs. Belva Lockwood

1892

Grover Cleveland, president
Adlai E. Stevenson, vice-president

> Others receiving votes: Benjamin Harrison, James B. Weaver, John Bidwell, Simon Wing

1896

William McKinley, president
Garret A. Hobart, vice-president

> Others receiving votes: William J. Bryan, John M. Palmer, Joshua Levering, Charles H. Matchett, Charles E. Bentley

1900

William McKinley, president
Theodore Roosevelt, vice-president

> Others receiving votes: William J. Bryan, John G. Wooley, Eugene Debs, Job Harriman, Joseph F. Malloney, Wharton Barker, Donelson Laffery, Seth B. Ellis, Jonah F. Leonard

1904

Theodore Roosevelt, president
Charles W. Fairbanks, vice-president

> Others receiving votes: Alton B. Parker, Silas C. Swallow, Eugene Debs, Charles H. Corrigan, Thomas E. Watson, George E. Taylor, Austin H. Holcomb

1908

William H. Taft, president
James S. Sherman, vice-president

> Others receiving votes: William J. Bryan, Eugene W. Chafin, Eugene V. Debs, August Gillhaus, Thomas E. Watson, Thomas L. Hisgen, W.R. Benkert, Daniel B. Turney

1912

Woodrow Wilson, president
Thomas R. Marshall, vice-president

> Others receiving votes: Theodore Roosevelt, William Howard Taft, Eugene V. Debs, Eugene W. Chafin, Arthur E. Reimer, Blauford F. Ziggfeld

1916

Woodrow Wilson, president
Thomas R. Marshall, vice-president

> Others receiving votes: Charles Evans Hughes, Allan L. Benson, James F. Hanley, Hollister Purdue, Arthur E. Reimer

1920

Warren G. Harding, president
Calvin Coolidge, vice-president

> Others receiving votes: James M. Cox, Aaron S. Watkins, Parley P. Christensen, Eugene V. Debs, William W. Cox, Robert C. Macauley, James E. Ferguson

1924

Calvin Coolidge, president
Charles G. Dawes, vice-president

> Others receiving votes: John W. Davis, Herman P. Faris, William Z. Foster, Frank T. Johns, Robert M. LaFollette, William Wallace, John Zahnd, Gilbert Nations, Jacob S. Coxey, Benson A. Cropp

1928

Herbert Hoover, president
Charles Curtis, vice-president

> Others receiving votes: Alfred E. Smith, Norman Thomas, William Z. Foster, Verne L. Reynolds, William Varney, Frank Webb, John Zahnd, Wilcox Rondo, Dr. Henry Hoffman

1932

Franklin D. Roosevelt, president
John N. Garner, vice-president

> Others receiving votes: Herbert Hoover, Norman Thomas, William Z. Foster, William D. Upshaw, William H. Harvey, Verne L. Reynolds, Jacob S. Coxey, John Zahnd, James R. Cox, Laven Keshibian

1936

Franklin D. Roosevelt, president
John N. Garner, vice-president

> Others receiving votes: Alfred M. Landon, William Lemke, Norman Thomas, Earl Russell Browder, David Leigh Colvin, John W. Aiken, William Pelley, John Zahnd

1940

Franklin D. Roosevelt, president
Henry A. Wallace, vice-president

> Others receiving votes: Wendell Willkie, Norman Thomas, Roger Ward Babson, Earl Russell Browder, John W. Aiken, Alfred Knutson, John Zahnd, Anna Milburn

1944

Franklin D. Roosevelt, president
Harry S. Truman, vice-president

> Others receiving votes: Thomas E. Dewey, Norman Thomas, Claude A. Watson, Edward A. Teichert, Gerald L.K. Smith

1948

Harry S. Truman, president
Alben W. Barkley, vice-president

> Others receiving votes: Thomas E. Dewey, J. Strom Thurmond, Henry A. Wallace, Norman Thomas, Claude A. Watson, Edward A. Teichert, Farrell Dobbs, Gerald L.K. Smith, John G. Scott, John Maxwell

1952

Dwight D. Eisenhower, president
Richard M. Nixon, vice-president

Others receiving votes: Adlai E. Stevenson, Vincent Halliman, Stuart Hamblen, Eric Hass, Darlington Hoopes, Douglas A. MacArthur, Farrell Dobbs, Henry B. Krajewski, Homer Tomlinson, Frederick C. Proehl, Ellen L. Jensen, Daniel J. Murphy

1956

Dwight D. Eisenhower, president
Richard M. Nixon, vice-president

Others receiving votes: Adlai E. Stevenson, Walter B. Jones, T. Coleman Andrews, Harry F. Byrd, Eric Hass, Enoch Arden Holtwick, William Ezra Jenner, Farrell Dobbs, Darlington Hoopes, Henry B. Krajewski, Gerald L.K. Smith, Homer Tomlinson, Herbert Shelton, Frederick C. Proehl, William Langer

1960

John F. Kennedy, president
Lyndon B. Johnson, vice-president

Others receiving votes: Richard M. Nixon, Harry F. Byrd, Orval Faubus, Eric Hass, Rutherford L. Decker, Farrell Dobbs, Charles Loten Sullivan, Joseph Bracken Lee, C. Benton Coiner, Lar Daly, Clennon King, Merritt Barton Curtis, Symon Gould, Whitney Hart Slocum, Homer Tomlinson, T. Coleman Andrews

1964

Lyndon B. Johnson, president
Hubert H. Humphrey, vice-president

Others receiving votes: Barry M. Goldwater, Eric Hass, Clifton DeBerry, Earle Harold Munn, John Kaspar, Joseph B. Lightburn, Kirby Hensley, Homer Tomlinson, T. Coleman Andrews, Yette Bronstein, D.X.B. Schwartz, Louis E. Jaeckel

1968

Richard M. Nixon, president
Spiro Agnew, vice-president

Others receiving votes: Hubert H. Humphrey, George C. Wallace, Henning A. Blumen, Dick Gregory, Fred Halstead, Eldridge Cleaver, Eugene McCarthy, Earle Harold Munn, Charlene Mitchell

1972

Richard M. Nixon, president
Spiro Agnew, vice-president

Others receiving votes: George McGovern, John G. Schmitz, Linda Jenness, Benjamin Spock, Louis Fisher, Gus Hall, Harold Munn, John Hospers, John Mahalchik, Edward Wallace, Gabriel Green

On October 10, 1973, Spiro Agnew resigned as vice-president. On August 8, 1974, Richard Nixon announced his resignation as president of the United States. After the resignation of Agnew, Gerald R. Ford was confirmed as vice-president on December 6, 1973. He was elevated to the presidency on August 9, 1974, following Nixon's resignation. Nelson Rockefeller was nominated for the vice-presidency on August 20, 1974, and began his term December 19, 1974. His appointment came as a result of Ford's succeeding to the presidency.

1976

Jimmy Carter, president
Walter Mondale, vice-president

Others receiving votes: Gerald R. Ford, Eugene McCarthy, Roger McBride, Lester G. Maddox, Thomas Anderson, Peter Camejo, Gus Hall, Margaret Wright, Lyndon H. LaRouche, Benjamin C. Bubar, Jules Levin, Frank P. Zeidler

1980

Ronald Reagan, president
George Bush, vice-president

Others receiving votes: Jimmy Carter, John Rarick, Edward Clark, John Anderson, David McReynolds, Clifford DeBerry, Gus Hall, Barry Commoner, Deidre Griswold

Bibliography

American Glass from the Pages of Antiques: II Pressed and Cut. Princeton, New Jersey: Pyne Press, 1974.

American Heritage, Volume XIII, Number 5. New York: American Heritage Publishing Co., 1962.

American Heritage Auction of Americana Catalogue, Volumes I and II. New York: Sotheby, Parke, Bernet, Inc., 1979.

American Heritage Book of the Presidents and Famous Americans, Volumes I through VIII. New York: American Heritage Publishing Co., 1967.

Betts, John L., and Allen, Jack. *History U.S.A.* New York: American Book Co., 1967.

Brown, Joseph G. *The Nation's Choice.* Milwaukee, Wisconsin: Association Corp., 1972.

Cloak, Evelyn Campbell. *Glass Paperweights of the Bergstrom Art Center.* New York: Crown Publishers, Inc., 1966.

Ferson, Regis F., and Ferson, Mary F. *Yesterday's Milk Glass Today.* Pittsburgh, Pennsylvania: Regis F. and Mary F. Ferson, 1981.

Freidel, Frank. *The Presidents of the United States of America.* Washington, D.C.: White House Historical Association, 1964.

Gores, Stan. *1876 Centennial Collectibles.* Fond du Lac, Wisconsin: Haber Printing Co., 1974.

Hake, Theodore L. *Political Buttons, Book II, 1920-1976, Political Buttons, Book III, 1789-1916.* York, Pennsylvania: Hakes Americana and Collectibles Press, 1977-1978.

Kahler, James G. *Hail to the Chief.* Princeton, New Jersey: The Pyne Press, 1972.

Kane, Joseph N. *Facts About the Presidents.* New York: Charter Communications, 1976.

Klamkin, Marian. *American Patriotic and Political China.* New York: Charles Scribner's Sons, 1973.

Kovel, Ralph, and Kovel, Terry. *The Kovel's Complete Antiques Price List, Tenth Edition.* New York: Crown Publishers, Inc., 1977.

Lindsey, Bessie M. *American Historical Glass.* Rutland, Vermont: Charles E. Tuttle and Co., 1967.

Marsh, Tracy. *The American Story Recorded in Glass.* Minneapolis, Minnesota: Tracy Marsh, 1962.

McKearin, George P., and McKearin, Helen. *American Glass.* New York: Crown Publishers, Inc., 1948.

Morgan, H. Wayne. *From Hayes to McKinley, National Party Politics 1877-1896.* Syracuse, New York: Syracuse University Press, 1969.

Newton, Charles B., and Treat, Edwin B. *Outline for Review American History.* New York: American Book Co., 1907.

Official Associated Press Almanac 1973. New York: Almanac Publishing Co., Inc., 1972.

Patterson, Jerry E. *A Collectors Guide to Relics and Memorabilia.* New York: Crown Publishers, Inc., 1974.

Peters, Harry T. *Currier and Ives, Printmakers to the American People.* Garden City: Doubleday, Doran and Co., Inc., 1942.

Peterson, Arthur G. *Glass Patents and Patterns.* DeBary, Florida: Dr. Arthur G. Peterson, 1973.

Presidency, Special Issue, American Heritage Volume XV, Number 5. New York: American Heritage Publishing Co., 1964.

Presidential Elections Since 1789. Second Edition, Washington, D.C.: Congressional Quarterly, Inc., 1979.

Ray, Marcia. *Collectible Ceramics.* New York: Crown Publishers, Inc., 1974.

Russell, Francis. *The Shadow of Blooming Grove.* New York: McGraw-Hill Book Co., 1968.

Smithsonian Institution. *Every Four Years.* Washington, D.C.: Smithsonian Exposition Books, 1980.

Stefano, Frank, Jr. *Pictorial Souvenirs and Commemoratives of North America.* New York: E.P. Dutton Co., Inc., 1976.

Stuart, Anna Maude. *Bread Plates and Platters.* Hillsborough, California: Anna Maude Stuart, 1965.

Sullivan, Edmund B. *Collecting Political Americana.* New York: Crown Publishers, Inc., 1980.

United States Presidents. Indianapolis, Indiana: The Curtis Publishing Co., 1980.

Warman E.G. *Antiques and Their Prices,* Fifteenth Edition. Uniontown, Pennsylvania: E.G. Warman Publishing Co., 1980.

Warner, Don. *Collection of Political Memorabilia Catalogue.* Boston, Massachusetts: New England Rare Coin Auctions, 1981.

Wearin, Otha D. *Political Americana.* Shenandoah, Iowa: World Publishing Co., 1967.

Index

About the Author

For nearly twenty years, author Stan Gores and his wife, Jeannine, have sought mementos that are related to American presidents and events in American history. In the course of that time, they have assembled some outstanding collections.

In 1974, Gores wrote a book entitled, *1876 Centennial Collectibles and Price Guide* that sold out in two printings. But his major interest, as well as that of his wife, has been our American presidents and all the souvenirs made in their honor to promote their campaigns and to pay tribute to their days in the White House.

Gores has spent years researching the presidents, their lives, and the massive array of mementos that will immortalize them in the ranks of collectors. *Presidential and Campaign Memorabilia* is the result of that effort.

A graduate of Northwestern University's Medill School of Journalism, Gores has written for such magazines as *Ford Times, Yankee, Antiques Journal, Hobbies, The Spinning Wheel* and the scholarly *Wisconsin Magazine of History*. In addition, articles, columns, and stories he has written have appeared in three other books, the *Antique Trader,* and such newspapers as the *Chicago Tribune* and the *Philadelphia Bulletin*. More than a half dozen of his articles have been reprinted in the *Congressional Record*. His writing has earned him two national Freedoms Foundation Awards along with awards from the Wisconsin Newspaper Association, Wisconsin Association of School Boards, and the Wisconsin State Historical Society.

While he has been writing on presidential collectibles, Mrs. Gores has been lecturing and showing slides on the subject to a variety of clubs and antique organizations. Mr. and Mrs. Gores live in Fond du Lac, Wisconsin, located on the southern shores of Lake Winnebago, where they have raised eight children. He serves as managing editor of the Fond du Lac *Reporter*.